Joselyn Clark

FATTY LIVER DIET
COOKBOOK
FOR BEGINNERS

HEALTHY RECIPES TO NOURISH YOUR LIVER
AND TRANSFORM YOUR LIFESTYLE –
A BEGINNER'S GUIDE TO THE FAT LIVER COOKBOOK

CONTENTS

CHAPTER 1
UNDERSTANDING FATTY LIVER DISEASE

WHAT IS FATTY LIVER DISEASE?

Fatty Liver Disease, medically known as hepatic steatosis, is a condition characterized by the accumulation of fat in the liver cells. This buildup of fat can impair liver function and lead to inflammation, potentially progressing to more severe conditions like non-alcoholic fatty liver disease (NAFLD) or non-alcoholic steatohepatitis (NASH).

Types of Fatty Liver Disease

1. **Non-Alcoholic Fatty Liver Disease (NAFLD):** This is the most common form of fatty liver disease and is not related to excessive alcohol consumption. NAFLD covers a spectrum of conditions, ranging from simple fatty liver to more severe forms that can cause liver damage.

2. **Non-Alcoholic Steatohepatitis (NASH):** NASH is a more advanced stage of NAFLD characterized by liver inflammation and damage. It involves not only fat accumulation but also inflammation and liver cell damage, which can progress to fibrosis, cirrhosis, and even liver failure.

Causes and Risk Factors

- **Obesity and Metabolic Syndrome:** Excess weight, particularly around the abdomen, and conditions like insulin resistance, high blood sugar, high blood pressure, and abnormal cholesterol levels contribute significantly to fatty liver disease.

- **Unhealthy Diet:** Diets high in refined carbohydrates, sugars, saturated fats, and processed foods can increase the risk of developing fatty liver disease.

- **Insulin Resistance:** When the body's cells become resistant to insulin, it can lead to an increased accumulation of fat in the liver.

- **Type 2 Diabetes:** Individuals with diabetes are at a higher risk of developing fatty liver disease due to their body's impaired ability to regulate sugar levels.

- **Genetics:** Genetic factors can predispose some individuals to fatty liver disease, making them more susceptible even without other risk factors.

- **Medications and Toxins:** Certain medications, as well as exposure to toxins and pollutants, can contribute to liver damage and fat accumulation.

Understanding these aspects is crucial for beginners as it helps them comprehend the underlying causes and risk factors that contribute to the development and progression of fatty liver disease. This knowledge serves as a foundation for adopting dietary and lifestyle changes outlined in the Fatty Liver Diet Cookbook to manage and potentially reverse the condition.

THE IMPORTANCE OF DIET IN MANAGING FATTY LIVER

Impact of Diet on Liver Health

The liver plays a pivotal role in processing nutrients, metabolizing fats, and detoxifying the body. Diet directly influences liver health, impacting its ability to function optimally. Here's how:

- **Fat Accumulation:** Excessive intake of unhealthy fats and sugars can overload the liver, leading to the accumulation of fat within liver cells, a key factor in fatty liver disease.

- **Inflammation and Oxidative Stress:** Certain foods, especially those high in refined sugars and trans fats, can trigger inflammation and oxidative stress in the liver, worsening existing liver conditions.

- **Nutrient Deficiencies:** Inadequate intake of essential nutrients, such as antioxidants, vitamins, and minerals, can compromise the liver's ability to repair and regenerate, exacerbating liver damage.

Role of Nutrition in Fatty Liver Disease

- **Balancing Macronutrients:** A balanced diet comprising adequate protein, healthy fats (such as omega-3 fatty acids), and complex carbohydrates from whole grains, fruits, and vegetables supports liver health and aids in managing fatty liver disease.

- **Antioxidants and Phytonutrients:** Foods rich in antioxidants (like berries, leafy greens, and nuts) and phytonutrients (found in colorful fruits and vegetables) help combat oxidative stress and reduce inflammation in the liver.

- **Fiber and Gut Health:** High-fiber foods promote a healthy gut microbiome, aiding in digestion and reducing the absorption of fats, thereby easing the burden on the liver.

- **Limiting Harmful Substances:** Cutting back on alcohol, refined sugars, trans fats, and processed foods is crucial in preventing further liver damage and supporting its healing process.

Understanding the direct impact of diet on liver health empowers beginners to make informed choices when selecting foods for their Fatty Liver Diet. By focusing on nutrient-dense, liver-supportive foods and minimizing harmful dietary components, individuals can take a proactive approach to managing and potentially reversing fatty liver disease.

CHAPTER 2
PRINCIPLES OF THE FATTY LIVER DIET

THE FOUNDATION OF THE FATTY LIVER DIET

Establishing a solid foundation for the Fatty Liver Diet involves several key principles that form the basis for supporting liver health and managing fatty liver disease.

Balancing Macronutrients

Understanding and balancing macronutrients—proteins, carbohydrates, and fats—are crucial for a healthy Fatty Liver Diet.

- **Proteins:** Incorporate lean protein sources such as skinless poultry, fish, tofu, beans, legumes, and low-fat dairy products into your meals. Protein provides essential amino acids that aid in repairing liver cells, supporting liver function, and maintaining muscle mass.

- **Carbohydrates:** Focus on complex carbohydrates derived from whole grains like brown rice, quinoa, whole wheat products, as well as fruits and vegetables. These carbohydrates contain fiber, vitamins, and minerals, providing sustained energy and aiding in digestive health. Limit intake of simple sugars found in processed foods and sugary drinks, as they can contribute to liver fat accumulation.

- **Fats:** Choose healthy fats like those found in avocados, nuts, seeds, and olive oil. These fats contain omega-3 fatty acids and monounsaturated fats, which help reduce inflammation and support liver health. Minimize consumption of saturated fats found in red meat and processed foods, as well as trans fats commonly found in fried and packaged foods, as they can exacerbate liver damage.

Portion Control and Meal Timing

Portion control and meal timing play significant roles in managing fatty liver disease.

- **Portion Control:** Be mindful of portion sizes to prevent overloading the liver with excess calories. Use smaller plates, measure servings, and pay attention to hunger and fullness cues. Balancing portions helps manage weight and reduces the strain on the liver.

- **Meal Timing:** Aim for consistent meal times throughout the day, spacing meals at regular intervals to avoid prolonged periods without food. This routine helps regulate blood sugar levels, prevents excessive stress on the liver, and supports overall metabolic function. Avoid late-night heavy meals, allowing the liver ample time to rest and repair overnight.

Understanding and implementing these foundational aspects of the Fatty Liver Diet—balancing macronutrients and practicing portion control with strategic meal timing—empowers beginners to make informed dietary choices. These principles serve as the cornerstone for crafting a personalized diet plan that actively supports liver health and aids in managing fatty liver disease.

CHOOSING THE RIGHT FOODS

Liver-Friendly Foods

Selecting liver-friendly foods is paramount in managing fatty liver disease and promoting overall liver health.

- **Leafy Greens:** Spinach, kale, and other leafy greens are rich in antioxidants, vitamins, and minerals that support liver function and help in reducing inflammation.
- **Cruciferous Vegetables:** Broccoli, Brussels sprouts, and cauliflower contain compounds that aid in detoxification processes within the liver.
- **Berries:** Blueberries, strawberries, and raspberries are packed with antioxidants that combat oxidative stress and reduce liver inflammation.
- **Fatty Fish:** Salmon, mackerel, and sardines are excellent sources of omega-3 fatty acids, which have anti-inflammatory properties and support liver health.
- **Nuts and Seeds:** Walnuts, almonds, flaxseeds, and chia seeds are rich in healthy fats, antioxidants, and fiber, promoting liver function and reducing liver fat.
- **Green Tea:** Loaded with antioxidants, green tea helps protect liver cells from damage and supports overall liver health.

Foods to Limit or Avoid

Certain foods can exacerbate fatty liver disease and should be limited or avoided to prevent further liver damage.

- **Added Sugars:** Sugary foods and beverages like sodas, candies, and processed sweets contribute to liver fat accumulation and inflammation.
- **Highly Processed Foods:** Processed foods containing refined grains, trans fats, and additives can burden the liver and worsen liver health.
- **Fatty and Fried Foods:** Deep-fried foods, as well as foods high in unhealthy fats like fast food, processed meats, and high-fat dairy products, should be minimized to reduce liver inflammation and fat buildup.
- **Excessive Alcohol:** Alcohol can cause liver inflammation and damage, so it's essential to limit or avoid alcohol entirely, especially for individuals with fatty liver disease.
- **Excessive Salt:** High-sodium foods can lead to fluid retention and may worsen conditions related to liver health. Monitoring salt intake is crucial.

By understanding which foods promote liver health and which to limit or avoid, beginners can proactively make dietary choices that support their liver while managing fatty liver disease. This knowledge forms the basis for designing a diet rich in liver-friendly foods and minimizing or eliminating those that could harm liver function.

CHAPTER 3
BUILDING A HEALTHY MEAL PLAN

Creating a balanced meal plan tailored to support liver health is essential in managing fatty liver disease effectively.

CREATING A BALANCED MEAL PLAN

Crafting a balanced meal plan involves incorporating liver-friendly foods while controlling portion sizes and meal frequency.

- **Balanced Plate Approach:** Aim for a well-rounded meal by including lean protein sources, whole grains, plenty of vegetables, and healthy fats in appropriate portions on your plate.

- **Frequent Meals:** Consider dividing your daily food intake into smaller, more frequent meals to prevent overloading the liver and maintain steady energy levels throughout the day.

- **Mindful Eating:** Practice mindful eating by paying attention to hunger and fullness cues. Avoid eating when not hungry and stop when comfortably satisfied.

Sample Meal Plan Ideas

Here are a few sample meal plan ideas that illustrate how to structure meals for a day:

1. **Breakfast:**

- *Option 1:* Greek yogurt topped with berries and a sprinkle of chia seeds.

- *Option 2:* Oatmeal made with almond milk, topped with sliced bananas and a handful of walnuts.

2. **Lunch:**

- *Option 1*: Grilled chicken salad with mixed greens, cherry tomatoes, cucumber, and olive oil vinaigrette.

- *Option 2:* Quinoa and black bean bowl with roasted vegetables and a side of steamed broccoli.

3. **Snack:**

- *Option 1:* Sliced apple with almond butter.

- *Option 2:* Carrot sticks with hummus.

4. **Dinner:**

- *Option 1:* Baked salmon with quinoa and sautéed spinach.

- *Option 2:* Stir-fried tofu with brown rice and a variety of colorful bell peppers.

Adjusting the Diet to Individual Needs

Individual needs can vary, so it's crucial to personalize the meal plan according to specific dietary preferences, allergies, and health conditions.

- Consultation with a Nutritionist: Seeking guidance from a nutritionist or healthcare professional can help tailor the diet plan to individual needs while ensuring nutritional adequacy.
- Food Allergies or Sensitivities: Adjust the meal plan by substituting foods that trigger allergies or sensitivities with suitable alternatives.
- Medical Conditions: Individuals with other medical conditions or specific dietary requirements should customize the meal plan to meet their unique health needs while supporting liver health.

By providing sample meal plan ideas and emphasizing the importance of personalization, beginners can grasp the concept of structuring meals to support liver health while accommodating individual preferences and requirements. This approach ensures a sustainable and effective Fatty Liver Diet that suits each person's specific needs.

TIPS FOR MEAL PREPARATION

Efficient meal preparation techniques and mindful cooking methods significantly contribute to a successful Fatty Liver Diet plan.

Cooking Methods for Liver Health

Choosing appropriate cooking methods can help preserve nutrients and minimize the use of unhealthy fats.

- Baking or Roasting: Opt for baking or roasting as these methods require minimal added fats while enhancing flavors. They help retain nutrients and produce delicious meals.
- Steaming and Boiling: Steaming vegetables or boiling them in minimal water preserves nutrients and avoids the need for added oils or fats.
- Sautéing with Healthy Fats: If sautéing, use small amounts of healthy fats like olive oil or avocado oil to cook vegetables or proteins at lower temperatures.
- Grilling or Broiling: Grilling or broiling meats and vegetables is a great way to add flavor without excessive fats. However, avoid charring or burning as it can produce harmful compounds.

Meal Prepping and Batch Cooking

Efficient meal prepping and batch cooking streamline the Fatty Liver Diet plan, making healthy eating more convenient.

- Plan Ahead: Design a weekly meal plan and create a shopping list to ensure you have all necessary ingredients on hand.
- Prep Ingredients in Advance: Wash, chop, and portion out ingredients like vegetables, fruits, and proteins in advance to save time during meal preparation.

- Batch Cooking: Cook larger quantities of meals and divide them into portions for multiple meals. Store these portions for quick and easy access to healthy, pre-made meals throughout the week.

- Use Freezer-Friendly Foods: Certain meals can be frozen for later use, making it easier to have a variety of healthy options available when time is limited.

By emphasizing suitable cooking methods that preserve nutrients and sharing strategies for efficient meal preparation, beginners can adopt practices that support liver health without sacrificing taste or convenience. These tips help individuals integrate the Fatty Liver Diet into their lifestyle seamlessly, promoting adherence and long-term success in managing fatty liver disease.

CHAPTER 4
NAVIGATING CHALLENGES
AND STAYING ON TRACK

Sticking to the Fatty Liver Diet can present challenges, but overcoming these obstacles is crucial for success in managing fatty liver disease.

OVERCOMING OBSTACLES IN ADHERING TO THE DIET

Recognizing and addressing common hurdles can help maintain consistency in following the Fatty Liver Diet.

- **Time Constraints:** Busy schedules can make meal preparation challenging. Plan ahead and use time-saving strategies like meal prepping and quick, healthy recipes.

- **Emotional Eating:** Stress or emotions might trigger unhealthy eating habits. Find alternative ways to manage stress, such as exercise, meditation, or hobbies, rather than turning to food for comfort.

- **Lack of Support:** Surround yourself with a supportive environment. Communicate your goals to friends and family, seek encouragement, or join support groups to stay motivated.

Dealing with Cravings and Temptations

Managing cravings and temptations is a crucial aspect of maintaining the Fatty Liver Diet.

- **Healthy Substitutions:** Substitute unhealthy cravings with healthier alternatives. For example, choose fruit instead of sugary snacks or air-popped popcorn instead of chips.

- **Mindful Indulgence:** Occasionally indulging in small portions of favorite treats can help satisfy cravings without derailing progress. Practice moderation and mindfulness.

- **Identify Triggers:** Recognize triggers that lead to cravings and find alternative coping mechanisms or distractions to overcome them.

Managing Social Situations and Dining Out

Social gatherings and dining out can pose challenges in adhering to the Fatty Liver Diet.

- **Plan Ahead:** Check restaurant menus in advance and look for healthier options. If possible, suggest restaurants that offer suitable choices for your dietary needs.

- **Communicate Your Needs:** Don't hesitate to inform hosts or restaurant staff about your dietary requirements. Most establishments are accommodating and can make adjustments upon request.

- **Focus on Socializing:** Redirect the focus of social gatherings away from food. Engage in conversations, activities, or outings that don't revolve solely around eating.

By addressing common obstacles, managing cravings, and offering strategies for social situations, beginners can navigate challenges more effectively while adhering to the Fatty Liver Diet. Empowering individuals with practical approaches helps them stay on track and achieve sustainable results in managing fatty liver disease.

MAINTAINING LONG-TERM LIVER HEALTH

Long-term liver health relies on consistent lifestyle changes, seeking support, and monitoring progress for sustained management of fatty liver disease.

Incorporating Lifestyle Changes

Adopting and maintaining healthy lifestyle habits complement the Fatty Liver Diet and contribute to long-term liver health.

- **Regular Exercise:** Engage in regular physical activity, aiming for at least 150 minutes of moderate exercise per week. Exercise helps in weight management, improves insulin sensitivity, and supports liver health.

- **Stress Management:** Practice stress-reducing activities like yoga, meditation, or mindfulness techniques. Chronic stress can impact liver health, so finding effective stress management strategies is crucial.

- **Adequate Sleep:** Prioritize quality sleep as inadequate sleep patterns can affect liver function. Aim for 7-9 hours of uninterrupted sleep each night.

Seeking Support and Monitoring Progress

Seeking support and tracking progress are essential for maintaining motivation and ensuring the effectiveness of the Fatty Liver Diet.

- **Healthcare Professional Guidance:** Regularly consult with healthcare professionals, including doctors and dietitians, to monitor liver health and receive guidance on diet and lifestyle adjustments.

- **Support Networks:** Join support groups or online communities where individuals share similar health concerns. Sharing experiences and tips can provide encouragement and motivation.

- **Monitoring Progress:** Keep track of dietary habits, physical activity, and overall well-being. Use tools like food journals or apps to monitor progress and identify areas for improvement.

By emphasizing the integration of healthy lifestyle changes, seeking professional support, and actively monitoring progress, beginners can establish habits that promote long-term liver health. These practices form the foundation for sustained management of fatty liver disease, leading to improved overall well-being.

CHAPTER 5
COMMON QUESTIONS AND ANSWERS

Addressing common queries helps beginners navigate the Fatty Liver Diet with clarity and confidence.

What is the role of exercise in managing fatty liver disease?

Exercise plays a crucial role in managing fatty liver disease by aiding in weight loss, improving insulin sensitivity, and reducing liver fat. Aim for at least 150 minutes of moderate exercise per week, incorporating activities like brisk walking, cycling, or swimming.

Can I have fruits if I have fatty liver disease?

Yes, fruits are generally healthy choices for individuals with fatty liver disease. They provide essential nutrients, fiber, and antioxidants. However, be mindful of portion sizes and choose whole fruits over fruit juices to avoid excessive sugar intake.

Is it okay to consume dairy products on the Fatty Liver Diet?

Moderate consumption of low-fat or non-fat dairy products, such as yogurt, milk, and cheese, can be part of a healthy Fatty Liver Diet. Opt for dairy products that are lower in saturated fats.

Can I drink coffee or tea while following the Fatty Liver Diet?

Moderate consumption of coffee and green tea is generally considered safe and may even have potential benefits for liver health due to their antioxidant properties. However, limit added sugars or high-fat additives in these beverages.

Are there specific foods I should avoid entirely if I have fatty liver disease?

Avoiding foods high in added sugars, trans fats, and highly processed foods is crucial in managing fatty liver disease. Minimize intake of sugary drinks, fast food, fried foods, and foods high in saturated fats.

What should I do if I experience cravings for unhealthy foods?

Substitute unhealthy cravings with healthier alternatives. Choose fruits, nuts, or air-popped popcorn instead of sugary or high-fat snacks. Practice moderation and mindfulness when occasionally indulging in favorite treats.

Can I follow the Fatty Liver Diet if I have other health conditions?

Consult with a healthcare professional or dietitian to tailor the Fatty Liver Diet to your specific health conditions or dietary needs. The diet can be adapted to accommodate various health concerns while supporting liver health.

Addressing these common questions offers beginners clarity and guidance when navigating the Fatty Liver Diet. Understanding these aspects empowers individuals to make informed decisions and successfully manage fatty liver disease while adhering to a healthy dietary regimen.

CHAPTER 6
COMMON MISTAKES
ON THE FATTY LIVER DIET

Identifying and addressing common mistakes can help beginners stay on track and maximize the effectiveness of the Fatty Liver Diet.

Overlooking Hidden Sugars and Unhealthy Additives

One common mistake is underestimating the presence of hidden sugars and unhealthy additives in processed foods, condiments, and sauces. Reading labels thoroughly and choosing whole, unprocessed foods can prevent inadvertently consuming harmful ingredients.

Excessive Focus on Specific Foods or Supplements

Focusing excessively on specific "superfoods" or supplements for liver health without considering overall dietary balance can lead to nutritional imbalances. Instead, aim for a varied diet rich in fruits, vegetables, lean proteins, and healthy fats.

Ignoring Portion Control

Neglecting portion control can undermine progress on the Fatty Liver Diet. Even healthy foods can contribute to weight gain if consumed in excessive amounts. Being mindful of portion sizes helps manage calorie intake and supports weight management.

Skipping Regular Physical Activity

Lack of regular exercise can hinder progress in managing fatty liver disease. Physical activity aids in weight management, improves insulin sensitivity, and supports liver health. Incorporating regular exercise into the routine is crucial for overall well-being.

Failure to Seek Professional Guidance

Not seeking guidance from healthcare professionals or dietitians can lead to misconceptions or improper diet planning. Consulting experts helps in crafting a personalized diet plan that aligns with individual needs and health conditions.

Rapid or Extreme Diet Changes

Adopting overly rapid or extreme diet changes can be unsustainable and potentially harmful. Gradual modifications to dietary habits are more likely to be maintained over the long term and support sustainable progress.

Inconsistency in following the Fatty Liver Diet can impede progress. Consistency in dietary habits, portion control, and lifestyle changes is key to achieving and maintaining improvements in liver health.

By understanding and rectifying these common mistakes, beginners can optimize their approach to the Fatty Liver Diet, ensuring adherence to healthy habits and maximizing the benefits for managing fatty liver disease.

CHAPTER 7
DELICIOUS RECIPES FOR A HEALTHY LIVER

BREAKFAST DELIGHTS

AVOCADO TOAST WITH SMOKED SALMON

Serving: 4 | Prep time: 10 minutes | Cook time: 5 minutes

Ingredients:

- 8 slices whole grain bread (1 oz each)
- 2 ripe avocados (8 oz total)
- 4 oz (113 g) smoked salmon
- 1 lemon
- 1 small red onion
- Fresh dill for garnish
- 1 tbsp olive oil
- Sea salt and black pepper

Directions:

1. Toast the whole grain bread slices to desired crispness.
2. While the bread is toasting, slice the avocados and red onion thinly.
3. Spread mashed avocado onto each toasted slice, layer with smoked salmon, and top with sliced red onion.
4. Squeeze fresh lemon juice on top, drizzle with a touch of olive oil, and sprinkle with sea salt, black pepper, and fresh dill.

Useful Tip: Opt for whole grain bread rich in fiber to increase its nutritional value.

Nutritional values: Calories: 250 kcal | Fat: 11 g | Protein: 15 g | Carbs: 23 g | Net carbs: 13 g | Fiber: 10 g | Cholesterol: 10 mg | Sodium: 450 mg | Potassium: 560 mg

QUINOA BREAKFAST BOWL WITH MIXED BERRIES

Serving: 4 | Prep time: 5 minutes | Cook time: 15 minutes

Ingredients:

- 8 oz (227 g) quinoa
- 16 oz (454 g) mixed berries (strawberries, blueberries, raspberries)
- 4 oz (113 g) almond butter
- 4 oz (113 g) unsweetened almond milk
- 2 oz (57 g) sliced almonds
- 1 oz (28 g) honey
- 1 tsp vanilla extract
- Fresh mint leaves for garnish

Directions:

1. Rinse the quinoa thoroughly and cook it according to package instructions.
2. In a small saucepan, heat the mixed berries over low heat until they release their juices, about 5-7 minutes.
3. In a separate saucepan, gently warm the almond butter, almond milk, honey, and vanilla extract over low heat until well combined.
4. Divide the cooked quinoa into bowls, top with the warm mixed berries, drizzle with the almond butter mixture, and sprinkle with sliced almonds.
5. Garnish with fresh mint leaves before serving.

Useful Tip: Adjust the sweetness by adding more or less honey based on personal preference.

Nutritional values: Calories: 340 kcal | Fat: 14 g | Protein: 9 g | Carbs: 46 g | Net carbs: 30 g | Fiber: 16 g | Cholesterol: 0 mg | Sodium: 80 mg | Potassium: 440 mg

SPINACH AND FETA OMELETTE

Serving: 4 | Prep time: 5 minutes | Cook time: 10 minutes

Ingredients:

- 8 large eggs
- 6 oz (170 g) fresh spinach, chopped
- 4 oz (113 g) crumbled feta cheese
- 2 oz (57 g) unsalted butter
- 1 oz (28 g) chopped green onions
- Salt and pepper to taste
- Fresh parsley for garnish
- Cooking spray

Directions:

1. In a bowl, whisk the eggs until well beaten and set aside.
2. In a non-stick skillet over medium-low heat, melt the butter and lightly coat the pan with cooking spray.
3. Add the chopped spinach and green onions to the skillet and sauté until the spinach wilts, approximately 2-3 minutes.
4. Pour the beaten eggs into the skillet, allowing them to spread evenly.
5. As the eggs begin to set, sprinkle the crumbled feta cheese over the omelette and season with salt and pepper.
6. Cook until the edges start to firm up and the center is almost set, about 3-4 minutes.
7. Carefully fold the omelette in half and continue cooking for an additional 2-3 minutes until fully set.
8. Slide the omelette onto a serving plate, garnish with fresh parsley, and serve hot.

Useful Tip: For a fluffier texture, add a tablespoon of milk or unsweetened almond milk while whisking the eggs.

Nutritional values: Calories: 270 kcal | Fat: 20 g | Protein: 17 g | Carbs: 4 g | Net carbs: 2 g | Fiber: 2 g | Cholesterol: 420 mg | Sodium: 410 mg | Potassium: 520 mg

MEDITERRANEAN VEGGIE SCRAMBLE

Serving: 4 | Prep time: 10 minutes | Cook time: 10 minutes

Ingredients:

- 8 large eggs
- 6 oz (170 g) cherry tomatoes, halved
- 4 oz (113 g) baby spinach
- 4 oz (113 g) crumbled goat cheese
- 2 oz (57 g) sliced black olives
- 1 oz (28 g) chopped red onion
- Fresh basil leaves for garnish
- Olive oil
- Salt and pepper to taste

Directions:

1. Heat a drizzle of olive oil in a non-stick skillet over medium heat.
2. Add the halved cherry tomatoes, sliced black olives, and chopped red onion to the skillet, sautéing until softened, about 2-3 minutes.
3. Add the baby spinach to the skillet and cook until wilted, approximately 1-2 minutes.
4. Meanwhile, crack the eggs into a bowl, whisk until well beaten, and season with salt and pepper.
5. Pour the beaten eggs into the skillet with the veggies, stirring gently with a spatula.
6. As the eggs begin to set, sprinkle in the crumbled goat cheese and continue stirring until the eggs are fully cooked but still moist and creamy, about 3-4 minutes.
7. Once cooked, transfer the scramble to a serving plate, garnish with fresh basil leaves, and serve hot.

Useful Tip: Add a dash of dried oregano or basil to enhance the Mediterranean flavors.

Nutritional values: Calories: 220 kcal | Fat: 15 g | Protein: 15 g | Carbs: 7 g | Net carbs: 4 g | Fiber: 3 g | Cholesterol: 380 mg | Sodium: 400 mg | Potassium: 450 mg

OATMEAL WITH CINNAMON APPLES AND WALNUTS

Serving: 4 | Prep time: 5 minutes | Cook time: 15 minutes

Ingredients:

- 2 oz (80 g) rolled oats
- 16 oz (473 ml) unsweetened almond milk
- 2 medium apples, peeled and diced
- 2 oz (57 g) chopped walnuts
- 1 tsp ground cinnamon
- 1 tbsp honey or maple syrup (optional)
- 1 tbsp olive oil

Directions:

1. Heat olive oil in a saucepan over medium heat.
2. Add diced apples to the pan and sauté for about 5-7 minutes until they start to soften.
3. Sprinkle ground cinnamon over the apples, stirring well to coat evenly.

4. In a separate pot, bring almond milk to a gentle boil, then add rolled oats.

5. Reduce heat and simmer for 5-7 minutes, stirring occasionally until the oats reach the desired consistency.

6. Once the oatmeal is cooked, divide it into serving bowls.

7. Top each bowl of oatmeal with the sautéed cinnamon apples and a sprinkle of chopped walnuts.

8. Drizzle with honey or maple syrup if desired.

Useful Tip: For added sweetness without using additional sweeteners, you can cook the apples with a splash of apple juice instead of olive oil.

Nutritional values: Calories: 280 kcal | Fat: 12 g | Protein: 7 g | Carbs: 38 g | Net carbs: 28 g | Fiber: 10 g | Cholesterol: 0 mg | Sodium: 80 mg | Potassium: 330 mg

SWEET POTATO HASH WITH TURKEY SAUSAGE

Serving: 4 | **Prep time:** 10 minutes | **Cook time:** 20 minutes

Ingredients:

- 12 oz (340 g) lean ground turkey sausage
- 2 medium sweet potatoes, peeled and diced
- 1 bell pepper, diced
- 1 onion, finely chopped
- 2 tbsp olive oil
- 1 tsp paprika
- Salt and pepper to taste
- Fresh parsley for garnish (optional)

Directions:

1. Heat olive oil in a large skillet over medium heat.

2. Add diced sweet potatoes to the skillet and cook for 8-10 minutes, stirring occasionally until they start to soften.

3. Add chopped onion and bell pepper to the skillet and cook for an additional 3-4 minutes until the vegetables are tender.

4. Push the vegetables to the side of the skillet and add the ground turkey sausage to the center, breaking it up with a spatula as it cooks.

5. Once the turkey sausage is fully cooked and browned, mix it with the cooked vegetables in the skillet.

6. Season the hash with paprika, salt, and pepper, stirring well to combine.

7. Cook for another 5-7 minutes until the sweet potatoes are cooked through and slightly crispy.

8. Garnish with fresh parsley if desired.

Useful Tip: For extra flavor, you can sprinkle a bit of grated Parmesan cheese over the hash before serving.

Nutritional values: Calories: 320 kcal | Fat: 18 g | Protein: 21 g | Carbs: 21 g | Net carbs: 16 g | Fiber: 5 g | Cholesterol: 60 mg | Sodium: 470 mg | Potassium: 700 mg

WHOLE GRAIN PANCAKES WITH BLUEBERRY COMPOTE

Serving: 4 | Prep time: 10 minutes | Cook time: 15 minutes

Ingredients:

- 8 oz (227 g) whole grain pancake mix
- 1 large egg
- 6 oz (170 g) fresh blueberries
- 2 tbsp water
- 1 tbsp maple syrup
- 1 tsp lemon zest
- 2 oz (57 g) chopped walnuts
- 1 tbsp olive oil

Directions:

1. Prepare the pancake batter by following the instructions on the pancake mix packaging, incorporating the egg into the mix.
2. In a saucepan over medium heat, combine the fresh blueberries, water, maple syrup, and lemon zest.
3. Cook the blueberry mixture for 8-10 minutes, stirring occasionally until the berries soften and break down slightly to form a compote-like consistency.
4. While the compote cooks, heat a non-stick skillet over medium heat and lightly grease it with olive oil.
5. Ladle the pancake batter onto the skillet to form pancakes of your desired size.
6. Cook the pancakes for 2-3 minutes on each side until they turn golden brown.
7. Serve the pancakes topped with the warm blueberry compote and a sprinkle of chopped walnuts.

Useful Tip: For extra fluffiness in pancakes, allow the pancake batter to rest for 5 minutes before cooking.

Nutritional values: Calories: 300 kcal | Fat: 12 g | Protein: 6 g | Carbs: 40 g | Net carbs: 35 g | Fiber: 5 g | Cholesterol: 45 mg | Sodium: 300 mg | Potassium: 200 mg

BREAKFAST BURRITO WITH BLACK BEANS AND SALSA

Serving: 4 | Prep time: 15 minutes | Cook time: 15 minutes

Ingredients:

- 8 large eggs
- 4 oz (113 g) black beans, drained and rinsed
- 4 oz (113 g) diced tomatoes
- 4 whole grain tortillas
- 2 oz (57 g) shredded cheddar cheese
- 1 oz (28 g) diced green chilies
- 4 oz (120 ml) low-fat sour cream
- 1 tbsp olive oil
- Salt and pepper to taste

Directions:

1. In a bowl, whisk the eggs, salt, and pepper until well beaten.
2. Heat olive oil in a skillet over medium heat and scramble the eggs until cooked through.

3. Warm the whole grain tortillas in the skillet or microwave.
4. Assemble the burritos by placing scrambled eggs, black beans, diced tomatoes, diced green chilies, and shredded cheddar cheese onto each tortilla.
5. Roll the tortillas, tucking in the sides as you go to form burritos.
6. Serve with a dollop of low-fat sour cream on top.

Useful Tip: Consider adding chopped avocado for extra creaminess and healthy fats.

Nutritional values: Calories: 380 kcal | Fat: 18 g | Protein: 24 g | Carbs: 30 g | Net carbs: 25 g | Fiber: 5 g | Cholesterol: 365 mg | Sodium: 520 mg | Potassium: 480 mg

VEGGIE-PACKED BREAKFAST FRITTATA

Serving: 4 | Prep time: 15 minutes | Cook time: 20 minutes

Ingredients:

- 8 large eggs
- 4 oz (113 g) mushrooms, sliced
- 4 oz (113 g) bell peppers, diced
- 4 oz (113 g) cherry tomatoes, halved
- 2 oz (57 g) spinach leaves
- 2 oz (57 g) shredded low-fat mozzarella cheese
- 2 tbsp olive oil
- 1/2 tsp dried thyme
- Salt and pepper to taste

Directions:

1. Preheat your oven to 350°F (175°C).
2. In a large ovenproof skillet, heat olive oil over medium heat.
3. Add mushrooms and bell peppers, cooking until they start to soften, about 3-4 minutes.
4. Add cherry tomatoes and spinach leaves, cooking until the spinach wilts, approximately 2 minutes.
5. In a bowl, whisk together eggs, dried thyme, salt, and pepper.
6. Pour the egg mixture over the veggies in the skillet. Sprinkle shredded mozzarella evenly on top.
7. Cook on the stovetop for 3-4 minutes until the edges begin to set.
8. Transfer the skillet to the preheated oven and bake for about 12-15 minutes until the frittata is set and the cheese melts and turns golden.
9. Remove from the oven, let it cool slightly, then slice into wedges.

Useful Tip: For added richness, you can use whole milk instead of water when whisking the eggs.

Nutritional values: Calories: 220 kcal | Fat: 15 g | Protein: 16 g | Carbs: 6 g | Net carbs: 4 g | Fiber: 2 g | Cholesterol: 390 mg | Sodium: 320 mg | Potassium: 420 mg

APPLE CINNAMON BUCKWHEAT PORRIDGE

Serving: 4 | Prep time: 5 minutes | Cook time: 20 minutes

Ingredients:

- 8 oz (227 g) buckwheat groats
- 32 oz (946 ml) unsweetened almond milk
- 2 medium apples, diced
- 2 tbsp maple syrup
- 2 tsp ground cinnamon
- 2 oz (57 g) chopped almonds
- 1 tbsp coconut oil
- 1 tsp vanilla extract

Directions:

1. Rinse the buckwheat groats thoroughly under running water.
2. In a saucepan, combine the buckwheat groats and almond milk. Bring it to a boil, then reduce the heat to a simmer and cook for about 15 minutes until the groats soften and absorb most of the liquid.
3. While the buckwheat cooks, in a separate skillet, melt coconut oil over medium heat.
4. Add diced apples, maple syrup, ground cinnamon, and vanilla extract to the skillet. Cook for about 5 minutes until the apples soften and become slightly caramelized.
5. Once the buckwheat is cooked, spoon it into bowls.
6. Top the buckwheat with the cooked cinnamon apples and a sprinkle of chopped almonds.

Useful Tip: For added sweetness without extra sugar, consider using ripe apples or adding a drizzle of honey.

Nutritional values: Calories: 280 kcal | Fat: 10 g | Protein: 8 g | Carbs: 40 g | Net carbs: 30 g | Fiber: 10 g | Cholesterol: 0 mg | Sodium: 180 mg | Potassium: 450 mg

APPLE WALNUT SPINACH SALAD

Serving: 4 | Prep time: 10 minutes | Cook time: 5 minutes

Ingredients:

- 8 oz (227 g) fresh baby spinach leaves
- 2 medium apples, thinly sliced
- 4 oz (113 g) chopped walnuts
- 2 tbsp olive oil
- 2 tbsp apple cider vinegar
- 1 tsp Dijon mustard
- 2 tsp honey
- Salt and pepper to taste

Directions:

1. In a large mixing bowl, combine the fresh baby spinach leaves, thinly sliced apples, and chopped walnuts.
2. In a separate small bowl, whisk together the olive oil, apple cider vinegar, Dijon mustard, honey, salt, and pepper to make the dressing.
3. Pour the dressing over the salad ingredients.
4. Gently toss the salad until the ingredients are evenly coated with the dressing.
5. Serve immediately as a healthy and refreshing salad option.

Useful Tip: To enhance the flavors, consider adding a sprinkle of crumbled low-fat cheese or a handful of dried cranberries to the salad.

Nutritional values: Calories: 280 kcal | Fat: 22 g | Protein: 5 g | Carbs: 20 g | Net carbs: 15 g | Fiber: 5 g | Cholesterol: 0 mg | Sodium: 50 mg | Potassium: 520 mg

CUCUMBER AND TOMATO HERB SALAD

Serving: 4 | Prep time: 15 minutes | Cook time: 0 minutes

Ingredients:

- 16 oz (454 g) cucumbers, thinly sliced
- 12 oz (340 g) tomatoes, diced
- 2 oz (57 g) red onion, thinly sliced
- 2 tbsp extra virgin olive oil
- 2 tbsp red wine vinegar
- 1 tbsp fresh lemon juice
- 0,5 oz (15 g) chopped fresh parsley
- Salt and pepper to taste

Directions:

1. In a large mixing bowl, combine the thinly sliced cucumbers, diced tomatoes, and thinly sliced red onion.
2. In a separate small bowl, whisk together the extra virgin olive oil, red wine vinegar, fresh lemon juice, chopped fresh parsley, salt, and pepper to make the dressing.

3. Pour the dressing over the salad ingredients.

4. Gently toss the salad until the ingredients are evenly coated with the dressing.

5. Refrigerate the salad for at least 10 minutes before serving to allow the flavors to meld.

Useful Tip: For a burst of added flavor, consider garnishing the salad with crumbled low-fat cheese or a handful of chopped nuts.

Nutritional values: Calories: 110 kcal | Fat: 7 g | Protein: 2 g | Carbs: 11 g | Net carbs: 8 g | Fiber: 3 g | Cholesterol: 0 mg | Sodium: 10 mg | Potassium: 470 mg

GRILLED ZUCCHINI AND CHICKPEA SALAD

Serving: 4 | Prep time: 15 minutes | Cook time: 10 minutes

Ingredients:

- 16 oz (454 g) zucchini, sliced lengthwise
- 8 oz (227 g) canned chickpeas, drained and rinsed
- 4 oz (113 g) cherry tomatoes, halved
- 2 tbsp olive oil
- 2 tbsp balsamic vinegar
- 1 tbsp fresh lemon juice
- 1 oz (28 g) fresh basil leaves, torn
- Salt and pepper to taste

Directions:

1. Preheat a grill or grill pan over medium-high heat.

2. In a bowl, toss the zucchini slices with a drizzle of olive oil, salt, and pepper.

3. Grill the zucchini slices for 3-4 minutes on each side until tender and grill marks appear. Remove from the grill and let them cool slightly.

4. In a separate large mixing bowl, combine the grilled zucchini, drained chickpeas, halved cherry tomatoes, torn fresh basil leaves, olive oil, balsamic vinegar, and fresh lemon juice.

5. Gently toss all the ingredients together until they are evenly coated with the dressing.

6. Season with additional salt and pepper if needed.

7. Let the salad sit for 5 minutes to allow the flavors to blend before serving.

Useful Tip: For added depth of flavor, consider adding a sprinkle of crumbled low-fat feta cheese or chopped nuts to the salad before serving.

Nutritional values: Calories: 180 kcal | Fat: 9 g | Protein: 6 g | Carbs: 20 g | Net carbs: 15 g | Fiber: 5 g | Cholesterol: 0 mg | Sodium: 150 mg | Potassium: 550 mg

ORANGE ALMOND QUINOA SALAD

Serving: 1 | Prep time: 15 minutes | Cook time: 15 minutes

Ingredients:

- 8 oz (227 g) quinoa, cooked and cooled
- 4 oz (113 g) almonds, chopped
- 2 large oranges, segmented
- 2 oz (57 g) baby spinach leaves
- 2 tbsp olive oil
- 1 tbsp fresh lemon juice
- 1 tsp honey
- Salt and pepper to taste

Directions:

1. In a large mixing bowl, combine the cooked and cooled quinoa, chopped almonds, segmented oranges, and baby spinach leaves.
2. In a separate small bowl, whisk together the olive oil, fresh lemon juice, honey, salt, and pepper to create the dressing.
3. Drizzle the dressing over the salad ingredients.
4. Gently toss the salad until all the ingredients are evenly coated with the dressing.
5. Let the salad sit for 5 minutes to allow the flavors to meld before serving.

Useful Tip: For an extra burst of freshness, add a handful of chopped mint leaves or a sprinkle of zest from the orange before tossing the salad.

Nutritional values: Calories: 280 kcal | Fat: 16 g | Protein: 8 g | Carbs: 30 g | Net carbs: 25 g | Fiber: 5 g | Cholesterol: 0 mg | Sodium: 10 mg | Potassium: 480 mg

POMEGRANATE ARUGULA SALAD

Serving: 4 | Prep time: 15 minutes | Cook time: 0 minutes

Ingredients:

- 6 oz (170 g) baby arugula leaves
- 2 pomegranates, seeds extracted
- 4 oz (113 g) goat cheese, crumbled
- 2 oz (57 g) walnuts, chopped
- 2 tbsp balsamic vinegar
- 1 tbsp extra virgin olive oil
- 1 tbsp honey
- Salt and pepper to taste

Directions:

1. In a large mixing bowl, toss the baby arugula leaves, pomegranate seeds, crumbled goat cheese, and chopped walnuts gently.
2. In a small bowl, whisk together the balsamic vinegar, extra virgin olive oil, honey, salt, and pepper to create the dressing.
3. Drizzle the dressing over the salad ingredients in the mixing bowl.
4. Gently toss the salad until all the ingredients are evenly coated with the dressing.

For added crunch, toast the walnuts in a dry skillet over medium heat for a few minutes before adding them to the salad.

Nutritional values: Calories: 220 kcal | Fat: 16 g | Protein: 8 g | Carbs: 18 g | Net carbs: 14 g | Fiber: 4 g | Cholesterol: 10 mg | Sodium: 180 mg | Potassium: 350 mg

ROASTED CARROT AND LENTIL SALAD

Serving: 4 | Prep time: 15 minutes | Cook time: 25 minutes

Ingredients:

- 12 oz (340 g) carrots, peeled and sliced
- 6 oz (170 g) dry lentils, rinsed
- 2 oz (57 g) baby spinach leaves
- 2 tbsp olive oil
- 1 oz (28 g) chopped parsley
- 1 oz (28 g) feta cheese, crumbled
- 1 tbsp balsamic vinegar
- 1 tbsp honey
- Salt and pepper to taste

Directions:

1. Preheat the oven to 400°F (200°C). Toss the sliced carrots with 1 tbsp of olive oil and spread them on a baking sheet. Roast for 20-25 minutes until tender and slightly caramelized.

2. In a pot, cook the lentils according to package instructions until they are tender but not mushy. Drain any excess water and let them cool slightly.

3. In a large bowl, combine the roasted carrots, cooked lentils, baby spinach leaves, chopped parsley, and crumbled feta cheese.

4. In a small bowl, whisk together the remaining 1 tbsp of olive oil, balsamic vinegar, salt, and pepper and honey to create the dressing.

5. Drizzle the dressing over the salad and gently toss everything together until well combined.

Useful Tip: For added flavor, you can toss the cooked lentils with a pinch of cumin or paprika before combining them with the other salad ingredients.

Nutritional values: Calories: 280 kcal | Fat: 11 g | Protein: 12 g | Carbs: 35 g | Net carbs: 29 g | Fiber: 6 g | Cholesterol: 10 mg | Sodium: 180 mg | Potassium: 780 mg

PEAR AND WALNUT MIXED GREENS SALAD

Serving: 1 | Prep time: 15 minutes | Cook time: 5 minutes

Ingredients:

- 6 oz (170 g) mixed salad greens
- 2 pears, sliced
- 3 oz (85 g) walnuts, roughly chopped
- 2 oz (57 g) feta cheese, crumbled
- 1 oz (28 g) red onion, thinly sliced
- 2 tbsp olive oil
- 2 tbsp balsamic vinegar
- 1 tbsp honey
- Salt and pepper to taste

Directions:

1. In a dry skillet over medium heat, toast the walnuts for 4-5 minutes, stirring frequently until lightly golden. Remove from heat and let them cool.
2. In a large mixing bowl, combine the mixed greens, sliced pears, toasted walnuts, crumbled feta cheese, and thinly sliced red onion.
3. In a small bowl, whisk together the olive oil, balsamic vinegar, salt, pepper and honey to create the dressing.
4. Drizzle the dressing over the salad and gently toss until everything is evenly coated.

Useful Tip: If you prefer a sweeter taste, you can briefly marinate the sliced red onions in the dressing for 10-15 minutes before adding them to the salad.

Nutritional values: Calories: 250 kcal | Fat: 19 g | Protein: 5 g | Carbs: 20 g | Net carbs: 14 g | Fiber: 6 g | Cholesterol: 10 mg | Sodium: 180 mg | Potassium: 320 mg

BROCCOLI CRANBERRY SLAW WITH CITRUS DRESSING

Serving: 4 | Prep time: 15 minutes | Cook time: 0 minutes

Ingredients:

- 10 oz (283 g) broccoli florets, finely chopped
- 3 oz (85 g) dried cranberries
- 2 oz (57 g) sunflower seeds
- 2 oz (57 g) Greek yogurt
- 2 tbsp orange juice
- 1 tbsp lemon juice
- 1 tbsp honey
- 1 tbsp olive oil
- Salt and pepper to taste

Directions:

1. In a mixing bowl, combine the finely chopped broccoli florets, dried cranberries, and sunflower seeds.
2. In a separate bowl, whisk together the Greek yogurt, orange juice, lemon juice, honey, salt, pepper and olive oil to prepare the citrus dressing.
3. Pour the citrus dressing over the broccoli mixture and toss well until evenly coated.

To enhance flavors, let the slaw sit in the refrigerator for 15-20 minutes before serving to allow the flavors to meld together.

Nutritional values: Calories: 210 kcal | Fat: 12 g | Protein: 6 g | Carbs: 25 g | Net carbs: 18 g | Fiber: 7 g | Cholesterol: 2 mg | Sodium: 30 mg | Potassium: 460 mg

BEETROOT AND GOAT CHEESE SALAD

Serving: 4 | Prep time: 15 minutes | Cook time: 0 minutes

Ingredients:

- 14 oz (397 g) cooked and sliced beetroots
- 3 oz (85 g) mixed salad greens
- 4 oz (113 g) goat cheese, crumbled
- 2 tbsp extra virgin olive oil
- 1 tbsp balsamic vinegar
- 1 tbsp honey
- 1 oz (28 g) chopped walnuts
- Salt and pepper to taste

Directions:

1. Arrange the mixed salad greens on a serving plate and top them with the cooked and sliced beetroots.
2. Scatter the crumbled goat cheese over the beetroots.
3. In a small bowl, whisk together the extra virgin olive oil, balsamic vinegar, and honey to create the dressing.
4. Drizzle the dressing over the salad, ensuring even coverage.
5. Sprinkle the chopped walnuts on top and season with salt and pepper to taste.

Useful Tip: For added freshness, toss the salad with the dressing just before serving to preserve the crispness of the greens.

Nutritional values: Calories: 220 kcal | Fat: 16 g | Protein: 9 g | Carbs: 14 g | Net carbs: 12 g | Fiber: 2 g | Cholesterol: 15 mg | Sodium: 190 mg | Potassium: 430 mg

MINTY WATERMELON FETA SALAD

Serving: 4 | Prep time: 15 minutes | Cook time: 0 minutes

Ingredients:

- 24 oz (680 g) watermelon, cubed
- 4 oz (113 g) feta cheese, crumbled
- 2 tbsp extra virgin olive oil
- 2 tbsp balsamic vinegar
- 2 tbsp freshly squeezed lime juice
- 0,5 oz (15 g) fresh mint leaves, chopped
- 2 oz (57 g) arugula leaves
- 1 oz (28 g) sliced almonds

Directions:

1. In a large mixing bowl, combine the watermelon cubes, crumbled feta cheese, arugula leaves, and sliced almonds.

2. In a separate small bowl, whisk together the extra virgin olive oil, balsamic vinegar, and freshly squeezed lime juice to create the dressing.

3. Drizzle the dressing over the watermelon mixture, ensuring even coating.

4. Sprinkle the chopped fresh mint leaves on top for a refreshing finish.

Useful Tip: To keep the salad crisp, dress it just before serving to maintain the crunch of the ingredients.

Nutritional values: Calories: 180 kcal | Fat: 12 g | Protein: 5 g | Carbs: 15 g | Net carbs: 13 g | Fiber: 2 g | Cholesterol: 20 mg | Sodium: 250 mg | Potassium: 320 mg

SNACKS AND TREATS

BAKED SWEET POTATO CHIPS

Serving: 4 | Prep time: 10 minutes | Cook time: 25 minutes

Ingredients:

- 2 medium sweet potatoes (12 oz / 340 g), thinly sliced
- 2 tbsp olive oil
- 1/2 tsp paprika
- 1/2 tsp garlic powder
- Salt and pepper to taste
- Fresh rosemary sprigs for garnish
- Cooking spray

Directions:

1. Preheat the oven to 375°F (190°C) and line baking sheets with parchment paper, lightly coated with cooking spray.
2. In a large bowl, toss the thinly sliced sweet potatoes with olive oil, paprika, garlic powder, salt, and pepper until evenly coated.
3. Arrange the sweet potato slices in a single layer on the prepared baking sheets.
4. Bake for 10 minutes, then flip the slices and continue baking for an additional 10-15 minutes until they turn golden and crispy.
5. Remove from the oven and let the chips cool for a few minutes before serving.
6. Garnish with fresh rosemary sprigs for added aroma and flavor.

Useful Tip: For a crispier texture, ensure the sweet potato slices are evenly thin and spread out on the baking sheets.

Nutritional values: Calories: 110 kcal | Fat: 5 g | Protein: 1 g | Carbs: 16 g | Net carbs: 13 g | Fiber: 3 g | Cholesterol: 0 mg | Sodium: 70 mg | Potassium: 240 mg

ALMOND BUTTER PEACHES BITES

Serving: 4 | Prep time: 15 minutes | Cook time: 0 minutes

Ingredients:

- 2 ripe peaches (14 oz / 400 g), sliced
- 4 tbsp almond butter
- 2 tbsp chopped almonds
- 1 tbsp honey
- 1 tbsp lemon juice
- 1 oz (28 g) dark chocolate chips
- 1 tbsp unsweetened almond milk
- 1/2 tsp ground cinnamon

Directions:

1. Arrange the peach slices on a plate and drizzle with lemon juice to prevent browning.
2. Spread almond butter onto each peach slice.

3. In a separate bowl, mix chopped almonds, honey, almond milk and ground cinnamon.

4. Carefully sprinkle the almond-honey mixture over the almond buttered peaches.

5. Add a few dark chocolate chips on top of each slice.

6. Serve immediately or chill for 5-10 minutes for a refreshing treat.

Useful Tip: Ensure the peaches are ripe but firm to maintain texture and sweetness in these delightful bites.

Nutritional values: Calories: 130 kcal | Fat: 8 g | Protein: 3 g | Carbs: 15 g | Net carbs: 12 g | Fiber: 3 g | Cholesterol: 0 mg | Sodium: 10 mg | Potassium: 210 mg

ROASTED CABBAGE WITH HERBS

Serving: 4 | Prep time: 10 minutes | Cook time: 20 minutes

Ingredients:

- 1 medium-sized cabbage (28 oz / 800 g), sliced into wedges
- 2 tbsp olive oil
- 1 tbsp balsamic vinegar
- 2 cloves garlic, minced
- 1 tsp dried thyme
- 1 tsp dried rosemary
- Salt and pepper to taste
- Fresh parsley for garnish

Directions:

1. Preheat the oven to 400°F (200°C).

2. In a bowl, mix olive oil, balsamic vinegar, minced garlic, dried thyme, and rosemary.

3. Brush the cabbage wedges with this mixture, ensuring they're evenly coated.

4. Season with salt and pepper to taste.

5. Place the wedges on a baking sheet lined with parchment paper.

6. Roast in the preheated oven for 20 minutes or until the edges turn golden brown and the cabbage is tender.

7. Garnish with fresh parsley before serving.

Useful Tip: Adjust the cooking time based on your desired cabbage texture—some prefer it softer, while others enjoy a slight crunch.

Nutritional values: Calories: 110 kcal | Fat: 7 g | Protein: 2 g | Carbs: 12 g | Net carbs: 7 g | Fiber: 5 g | Cholesterol: 0 mg | Sodium: 40 mg | Potassium: 320 mg

COTTAGE CHEESE STUFFED BELL PEPPERS

Serving: 4 | Prep time: 15 minutes | Cook time: 25 minutes

Ingredients:

- 4 large bell peppers, halved and deseeded
- 14 oz (400 g) cottage cheese
- 1 medium zucchini (6 oz / 170 g), diced
- 1 small onion (3 oz / 85 g), finely chopped
- 2 cloves garlic, minced
- 2 tbsp olive oil
- 1 tsp dried oregano
- Salt and pepper to taste

Directions:

1. Preheat the oven to 375°F (190°C).
2. In a skillet over medium heat, add olive oil, onions, and garlic. Sauté until onions turn translucent.
3. Add diced zucchini to the skillet and cook for 5 minutes until softened. Remove from heat.
4. In a mixing bowl, combine the sautéed vegetables with cottage cheese, dried oregano, salt, and pepper. Mix well.
5. Stuff each bell pepper half with the cottage cheese mixture, filling them evenly.
6. Place the stuffed bell peppers on a baking dish.
7. Bake in the preheated oven for 25 minutes until the peppers are tender and the filling is lightly browned.
8. Garnish with fresh herbs if desired before serving.

Useful Tip: For added flavor, sprinkle a little grated Parmesan cheese over the stuffed peppers before baking.

Nutritional values: Calories: 180 kcal | Fat: 9 g | Protein: 12 g | Carbs: 12 g | Net carbs: 8 g | Fiber: 4 g | Cholesterol: 15 mg | Sodium: 550 mg | Potassium: 600 mg

VEGGIE STICKS WITH HUMMUS DIP

Serving: 4 | Prep time: 15 minutes | Cook time: 0 minutes

Ingredients:

- 8 oz (225 g) carrots, cut into sticks
- 8 oz (225 g) cucumber, cut into sticks
- 8 oz (225 g) bell peppers, sliced
- 8 oz (240 g) hummus
- 2 tbsp olive oil
- 1 tsp lemon juice
- 1 tsp chopped parsley
- Salt and pepper to taste

Directions:

1. Wash and cut the carrots, cucumber, and bell peppers into sticks.
2. In a small bowl, mix the hummus with olive oil, lemon juice, chopped parsley, salt, and pepper until well combined.
3. Serve the veggie sticks on a platter alongside the hummus dip.

4. Enjoy this nutritious and flavorful snack!

Useful Tip: For extra flavor in the hummus, try adding a pinch of cumin or smoked paprika.

Nutritional values: Calories: 180 kcal | Fat: 12 g | Protein: 6 g | Carbs: 15 g | Net carbs: 10 g |
Fiber: 5 g | Cholesterol: 0 mg | Sodium: 450 mg | Potassium: 550 mg

FISH AND SEAFOOD RECIPES

LEMON HERB BAKED SALMON

Serving: 4 | Prep time: 15 minutes | Cook time: 15 minutes

Ingredients:

- 4 salmon fillets (4 oz / 113 g each)
- 2 tbsp olive oil
- 2 cloves garlic, minced
- Zest of 1 lemon
- 2 tbsp chopped fresh dill
- 1 tbsp lemon juice
- Salt and pepper to taste
- Lemon slices for garnish

Directions:

1. Preheat the oven to 400°F (200°C). Line a baking sheet with parchment paper.
2. Place the salmon fillets on the prepared baking sheet.
3. In a small bowl, mix together olive oil, minced garlic, lemon zest, chopped fresh dill, lemon juice, salt, and pepper.
4. Spoon the herb mixture over the salmon fillets, spreading it evenly.
5. Bake the salmon in the preheated oven for about 12-15 minutes, or until the salmon easily flakes with a fork.
6. Garnish with lemon slices and serve.

Useful Tip: To avoid overcooking, check the salmon at the 10-minute mark as cooking time can vary based on the thickness of the fillets.

Nutritional values: Calories: 280 kcal | Fat: 18 g | Protein: 25 g | Carbs: 2 g | Net carbs: 1 g | Fiber: 1 g | Cholesterol: 80 mg | Sodium: 70 mg | Potassium: 600 mg

GARLIC BUTTER SHRIMP SKEWERS

Serving: 4 | Prep time: 20 minutes | Cook time: 8 minutes

Ingredients:

- 1 lb (454 g) large shrimp, peeled and deveined
- 2 tbsp olive oil
- 4 cloves garlic, minced
- Zest of 1 lemon
- 2 tbsp unsalted butter, melted
- 1 tbsp fresh lemon juice
- 1 tbsp chopped fresh parsley
- Salt and pepper to taste
- Skewers

Directions:

1. Preheat the grill to medium-high heat.
2. In a bowl, combine olive oil, minced garlic, lemon zest, melted butter, lemon juice, chopped fresh parsley, salt, and pepper.

3. Thread the shrimp onto skewers, piercing them through the tail and the head.

4. Brush the garlic butter mixture onto both sides of the shrimp skewers.

5. Place the skewers on the preheated grill and cook for 3-4 minutes on each side, or until the shrimp turns pink and slightly opaque.

6. Remove the shrimp skewers from the grill and serve hot.

Useful Tip: Soak wooden skewers in water for about 20-30 minutes before using them to prevent burning on the grill.

Nutritional values: Calories: 180 kcal | Fat: 10 g | Protein: 20 g | Carbs: 2 g | Net carbs: 1 g | Fiber: 1 g | Cholesterol: 190 mg | Sodium: 250 mg | Potassium: 220 mg

HERBED TILAPIA FILLETS

Serving: 4 | Prep time: 10 minutes | Cook time: 12 minutes

Ingredients:

- 4 tilapia fillets (approx. 4 oz each)
- 2 tbsp olive oil
- 2 cloves garlic, minced
- 1 tbsp lemon juice
- 1 tsp dried thyme
- 1 tsp dried oregano
- 1 tsp dried parsley
- Salt and pepper to taste

Directions:

1. Preheat the oven to 400°F (200°C).
2. Pat dry the tilapia fillets and place them in a baking dish.
3. In a small bowl, mix olive oil, minced garlic, lemon juice, dried thyme, dried oregano, dried parsley, salt, and pepper.
4. Brush the herb mixture evenly over the tilapia fillets.
5. Bake in the preheated oven for 10-12 minutes or until the fish is opaque and flakes easily with a fork.
6. Serve the herbed tilapia fillets hot.

Useful Tip: To prevent the fish from sticking to the baking dish, line it with parchment paper or lightly grease it before placing the fillets.

Nutritional values: Calories: 180 kcal | Fat: 8 g | Protein: 23 g | Carbs: 1 g | Net carbs: 0 g | Fiber: 1 g | Cholesterol: 55 mg | Sodium: 70 mg | Potassium: 460 mg

CITRUS GRILLED SWORDFISH

Serving: 4 | Prep time: 15 minutes | Cook time: 10 minutes

Ingredients:

- 4 swordfish fillets (about 4 oz each)
- 3 tbsp olive oil
- Zest of 1 lemon
- Zest of 1 orange
- 2 tbsp fresh lemon juice
- 2 tbsp fresh orange juice
- 1 tsp dried thyme
- Salt and pepper to taste

Directions:

1. Preheat your grill to medium-high heat (about 400°F/200°C).
2. In a bowl, mix olive oil, lemon zest, orange zest, lemon juice, orange juice, dried thyme, salt, and pepper.
3. Pat dry the swordfish fillets and brush both sides generously with the citrus mixture.
4. Grill the swordfish for about 4-5 minutes on each side or until cooked through and grill marks appear.
5. Once done, remove from the grill and let it rest for a couple of minutes before serving.

Useful Tip: To prevent the swordfish from sticking to the grill, make sure it's clean and well-oiled before placing the fillets.

Nutritional values: Calories: 250 kcal | Fat: 15 g | Protein: 26 g | Carbs: 2 g | Net carbs: 1 g | Fiber: 1 g | Cholesterol: 60 mg | Sodium: 70 mg | Potassium: 550 mg

POACHED COD WITH TOMATO SALSA

Serving: 4 | Prep time: 10 minutes | Cook time: 15 minutes

Ingredients:

- 4 cod fillets (about 5 oz each)
- 2 tbsp olive oil
- 1 tsp paprika
- Salt and pepper to taste
- 2 tomatoes, diced
- 1/2 red onion, finely chopped
- 2 oz (15 g) fresh cilantro, chopped
- Juice of 1 lime

Directions:

1. Pat dry the cod fillets and season both sides with salt, pepper, and paprika.
2. Heat olive oil in a skillet over medium heat.
3. Once hot, place the cod fillets in the skillet and cook for about 4-5 minutes on each side or until they're opaque and flaky.
4. Meanwhile, in a bowl, mix the diced tomatoes, chopped red onion, cilantro, lime juice, salt, and pepper to make the salsa.
5. Once the cod is cooked, remove it from the skillet and serve topped with the fresh tomato salsa.

For a more intense flavor, let the cod marinate in the olive oil and seasonings for 15-20 minutes before cooking.

Nutritional values: Calories: 220 kcal | Fat: 8 g | Protein: 30 g | Carbs: 5 g | Net carbs: 3 g | Fiber: 2 g | Cholesterol: 65 mg | Sodium: 150 mg | Potassium: 850 mg

OVEN-BAKED LEMON GARLIC TROUT

Serving: 4 | Prep time: 10 minutes | Cook time: 15 minutes

Ingredients:

- 4 trout fillets (about 4 oz each)
- 2 tbsp olive oil
- 2 cloves garlic, minced
- Zest of 1 lemon
- Juice of 1/2 lemon
- 1/4 tsp black pepper
- 1/4 tsp salt
- Fresh parsley, chopped for garnish

Directions:

1. Preheat the oven to 400°F (200°C).
2. Pat dry the trout fillets and place them on a parchment-lined baking sheet.
3. In a small bowl, mix olive oil, minced garlic, lemon zest, lemon juice, salt, and black pepper.
4. Brush the olive oil mixture onto each fillet, ensuring they are evenly coated.
5. Bake in the preheated oven for about 12-15 minutes or until the fish is opaque and flakes easily with a fork.
6. Once cooked, garnish with fresh chopped parsley and serve.

Useful Tip: For a delicate and moist texture, avoid overcooking the trout; it's best when it flakes easily but remains tender.

Nutritional values: Calories: 220 kcal | Fat: 12 g | Protein: 24 g | Carbs: 1 g | Net carbs: 0 g | Fiber: 1 g | Cholesterol: 70 mg | Sodium: 160 mg | Potassium: 450 mg

SESAME CRUSTED TUNA STEAKS

Serving: 4 | Prep time: 15 minutes | Cook time: 8 minutes

Ingredients:

- 4 tuna steaks (about 6 oz each)
- 1 oz (30 g) sesame seeds
- 2 tbsp soy sauce
- 1 tbsp olive oil
- 1 tsp rice vinegar
- 1 tsp honey
- 1 tsp grated ginger
- 1 clove garlic, minced

Directions:

1. Preheat the oven to 425°F (220°C).

2. In a shallow dish, spread sesame seeds and press tuna steaks into the seeds to coat both sides.

3. In a separate bowl, mix soy sauce, olive oil, rice vinegar, honey, grated ginger, and minced garlic.

4. Heat an oven-safe skillet over medium-high heat.

5. Sear the tuna steaks for 1-2 minutes on each side to get a golden crust.

6. Brush the soy sauce mixture onto the tops of the tuna steaks.

7. Transfer the skillet to the preheated oven and bake for 4-5 minutes for medium-rare, adjusting time for preferred doneness.

8. Once done, let the tuna rest for a couple of minutes before serving.

Useful Tip: Avoid overcooking; tuna steaks are best when slightly pink in the center for a tender, moist texture.

Nutritional values: Calories: 280 kcal | Fat: 12 g | Protein: 34 g | Carbs: 4 g | Net carbs: 3 g | Fiber: 1 g | Cholesterol: 65 mg | Sodium: 400 mg | Potassium: 500 mg

COCONUT LIME MAHI-MAHI

Serving: 4 | Prep time: 10 minutes | Cook time: 15 minutes

Ingredients:

- 4 Mahi-Mahi fillets (about 6 oz each)
- 2 oz (57 g) unsweetened coconut flakes
- 2 tbsp lime juice
- 1 tbsp olive oil
- 1 tbsp honey
- 1 tsp soy sauce
- 1/2 tsp grated ginger
- 1/2 tsp minced garlic

Directions:

1. Preheat the oven to 375°F (190°C).

2. In a bowl, mix together coconut flakes, lime juice, olive oil, honey, soy sauce, grated ginger, and minced garlic.

3. Pat dry the Mahi-Mahi fillets with paper towels and place them on a baking dish lined with parchment paper.

4. Spread the coconut mixture evenly over the fillets, gently pressing it down to coat.

5. Bake for 12-15 minutes until the fish is cooked through and the coconut is lightly toasted.

6. Serve the Mahi-Mahi hot, garnished with lime wedges if desired.

Useful Tip: Ensure the Mahi-Mahi is cooked just until it flakes easily with a fork; overcooking can make it dry.

Nutritional values: Calories: 320 kcal | Fat: 18 g | Protein: 34 g | Carbs: 8 g | Net carbs: 6 g | Fiber: 2 g | Cholesterol: 100 mg | Sodium: 240 mg | Potassium: 600 mg

BAKED HADDOCK WITH HERBED CRUST

Serving: 4 | Prep time: 15 minutes | Cook time: 20 minutes

Ingredients:

- 4 Haddock fillets (about 6 oz each)
- 2 oz (57 g) whole wheat breadcrumbs
- 2 tbsp chopped parsley
- 1 oz (28 g) grated Parmesan cheese
- 1 tbsp olive oil
- 1 tbsp lemon juice
- 1 tsp minced garlic
- Salt and pepper to taste

Directions:

1. Preheat the oven to 400°F (200°C).
2. In a bowl, combine breadcrumbs, chopped parsley, grated Parmesan cheese, olive oil, lemon juice, minced garlic, salt, and pepper.
3. Pat dry the Haddock fillets with paper towels and place them on a baking dish lined with parchment paper.
4. Spread the breadcrumb mixture evenly over the fillets, gently pressing it down to adhere.
5. Bake for 18-20 minutes until the crust is golden and the fish is cooked through.
6. Serve the Baked Haddock hot, garnished with fresh parsley or lemon wedges if desired.

Useful Tip: To avoid the crust from becoming soggy, ensure the fillets are dry before applying the breadcrumb mixture.

Nutritional values: Calories: 290 kcal | Fat: 10 g | Protein: 35 g | Carbs: 12 g | Net carbs: 10 g | Fiber: 2 g | Cholesterol: 90 mg | Sodium: 380 mg | Potassium: 600 mg

HERB-CRUSTED BAKED HALIBUT

Serving: 4 | Prep time: 10 minutes | Cook time: 15 minutes

Ingredients:

- 4 Halibut fillets (about 6 oz each)
- 2 oz (57 g) whole wheat breadcrumbs
- 1 oz (28 g) grated Parmesan cheese
- 1 oz (28 g) chopped fresh parsley
- 1 oz (28 g) chopped fresh chives
- 2 tbsp olive oil
- 1 tbsp lemon juice
- Salt and pepper to taste

Directions:

1. Preheat the oven to 400°F (200°C).
2. In a bowl, mix breadcrumbs, grated Parmesan cheese, chopped parsley, chopped chives, olive oil, lemon juice, salt, and pepper.
3. Pat dry the Halibut fillets with paper towels and place them on a baking dish lined with parchment paper.
4. Spread the herb and breadcrumb mixture evenly over the fillets, gently pressing it down to stick.

5. Bake for 12-15 minutes until the crust turns golden and the fish flakes easily with a fork.

6. Serve the Herb-Crusted Baked Halibut hot, garnished with fresh herbs or lemon wedges if desired.

Useful Tip: To maintain moisture in the fillets, brush them lightly with olive oil before applying the herb crust.

Nutritional values: Calories: 290 kcal | Fat: 12 g | Protein: 34 g | Carbs: 9 g | Net carbs: 7 g | Fiber: 2 g | Cholesterol: 70 mg | Sodium: 320 mg | Potassium: 550 mg

MEDITERRANEAN STYLE BAKED RED SNAPPER

Serving: 4 | Prep time: 15 minutes | Cook time: 20 minutes

Ingredients:

- 4 Red Snapper fillets (6 oz each)
- 2 oz (57 g) Kalamata olives, chopped
- 1 oz (28 g) sun-dried tomatoes, chopped
- 2 oz (57 g) whole wheat breadcrumbs
- 1 oz (28 g) grated Parmesan cheese
- 2 tbsp olive oil
- 1 tbsp lemon juice
- 2 cloves garlic, minced
- Salt and pepper to taste

Directions:

1. Preheat the oven to 375°F (190°C).

2. In a bowl, mix chopped olives, sun-dried tomatoes, breadcrumbs, grated Parmesan cheese, minced garlic, olive oil, lemon juice, salt, and pepper.

3. Pat dry the Red Snapper fillets and place them on a baking dish lined with parchment paper.

4. Divide the olive and breadcrumb mixture evenly over the fillets, pressing gently to adhere.

5. Bake for 18-20 minutes until the fish is cooked through and the crust turns golden brown.

6. Serve the Mediterranean Style Baked Red Snapper hot, garnished with fresh herbs or lemon wedges if desired.

Useful Tip: For added moisture, lightly brush the fillets with olive oil before applying the olive and breadcrumb mixture.

Nutritional values: Calories: 320 kcal | Fat: 15 g | Protein: 32 g | Carbs: 12 g | Net carbs: 8 g | Fiber: 4 g | Cholesterol: 75 mg | Sodium: 500 mg | Potassium: 600 mg

LEMON DILL STEAMED MUSSELS

Serving: 1 | Prep time: 10 minutes | Cook time: 8 minutes

Ingredients:

- 2 lbs (907 g) fresh mussels, cleaned and de-bearded
- 2 oz (57 g) unsalted butter
- 2 oz (60 ml) white wine
- 2 cloves garlic, minced
- 1 lemon, zest and juice
- 1 tbsp chopped fresh dill
- Salt and pepper to taste

Directions:

1. In a large pot with a lid, melt the butter over medium heat.
2. Add minced garlic and sauté until fragrant, about 1 minute.
3. Pour in the white wine, lemon juice, and lemon zest. Bring it to a gentle simmer.
4. Add cleaned mussels to the pot and cover with the lid. Cook for 5-6 minutes until the mussels open.
5. Sprinkle chopped fresh dill, salt, and pepper over the mussels. Gently toss to coat.
6. Serve the Lemon Dill Steamed Mussels hot with crusty whole grain bread to soak up the flavorful broth.

Useful Tip: Discard any mussels that remain closed after cooking, they might not be safe to eat.

Nutritional values: Calories: 230 kcal | Fat: 12 g | Protein: 18 g | Carbs: 8 g | Net carbs: 4 g | Fiber: 4 g | Cholesterol: 80 mg | Sodium: 500 mg | Potassium: 700 mg

BAKED LEMON PEPPER CATFISH

Serving: 4 | Prep time: 10 minutes | Cook time: 15 minutes

Ingredients:

- 4 catfish fillets (4 oz / 113 g each)
- 2 tbsp unsalted butter, melted
- 1 lemon, zest and juice
- 1 tbsp olive oil
- 2 tsp ground black pepper
- 1/2 tsp dried thyme
- Salt to taste
- Fresh parsley for garnish

Directions:

1. Preheat the oven to 375°F (190°C).
2. Pat dry the catfish fillets with a paper towel and place them in a baking dish.
3. In a bowl, mix melted butter, lemon zest, lemon juice, olive oil, ground black pepper, dried thyme, and a pinch of salt.
4. Drizzle the lemon-pepper mixture over the catfish fillets, ensuring they are evenly coated.
5. Bake in the preheated oven for 12-15 minutes or until the fish flakes easily with a fork.

6. Once done, garnish with fresh parsley and serve the Baked Lemon Pepper Catfish hot.

Useful Tip: To avoid overcooking, check the fish at the 12-minute mark; it should be opaque and easily flake with a fork.

Nutritional values: Calories: 240 kcal | Fat: 12 g | Protein: 25 g | Carbs: 2 g | Net carbs: 1 g | Fiber: 1 g | Cholesterol: 90 mg | Sodium: 100 mg | Potassium: 420 mg

BROILED HERB-MARINATED SEA BASS

Serving: 4 | Prep time: 15 minutes | Cook time: 12 minutes

Ingredients:

- 4 sea bass fillets (4 oz / 113 g each)
- 2 tbsp olive oil
- 2 tbsp fresh parsley, chopped
- 1 tbsp fresh dill, chopped
- 2 cloves garlic, minced
- 1 lemon, zest and juice
- Salt and pepper to taste
- Lemon wedges for serving

Directions:

1. Preheat the broiler in the oven.
2. In a bowl, combine olive oil, chopped parsley, chopped dill, minced garlic, lemon zest, lemon juice, salt, and pepper.
3. Pat dry the sea bass fillets and place them on a baking sheet lined with parchment paper.
4. Brush the herb-marinated mixture over the sea bass fillets, ensuring they are evenly coated.
5. Place the baking sheet under the broiler for about 10-12 minutes or until the fish is cooked through and easily flakes with a fork.
6. Once done, serve the Broiled Herb-Marinated Sea Bass with lemon wedges for an extra zest.

Useful Tip: Avoid overcooking; keep an eye on the fish while broiling to prevent it from drying out.

Nutritional values: Calories: 220 kcal | Fat: 10 g | Protein: 28 g | Carbs: 2 g | Net carbs: 1 g | Fiber: 1 g | Cholesterol: 70 mg | Sodium: 80 mg | Potassium: 470 mg

HERB ROASTED MONKFISH TAIL

Serving: 4 | Prep time: 15 minutes | Cook time: 20 minutes

Ingredients:

- 4 monkfish tail fillets (4 oz / 113 g each)
- 2 tbsp olive oil
- 2 tbsp fresh thyme leaves
- 2 tbsp fresh rosemary leaves
- 2 cloves garlic, minced
- 1 lemon, zest and juice
- Salt and pepper to taste
- Lemon wedges for serving

Directions:

1. Preheat the oven to 400°F (200°C).

2. In a bowl, mix olive oil, fresh thyme leaves, fresh rosemary leaves, minced garlic, lemon zest, lemon juice, salt, and pepper.

3. Place the monkfish tail fillets in a baking dish lined with parchment paper.

4. Spread the herb mixture evenly over the fillets, ensuring they are well coated.

5. Roast the monkfish tails in the preheated oven for about 18-20 minutes or until the fish is opaque and flakes easily with a fork.

6. Serve the Herb Roasted Monkfish Tail with lemon wedges for an added zing.

Useful Tip: Keep an eye on the cooking time to prevent overcooking, as monkfish can become dry if baked for too long.

Nutritional values: Calories: 220 kcal | Fat: 10 g | Protein: 30 g | Carbs: 2 g | Net carbs: 1 g | Fiber: 1 g | Cholesterol: 80 mg | Sodium: 90 mg | Potassium: 550 mg

HERB-ROASTED CHICKEN BREAST

Serving: 4 | Prep time: 10 minutes | Cook time: 25 minutes

Ingredients:

- 4 boneless, skinless chicken breasts (4 oz / 113 g each)
- 2 tbsp olive oil
- 2 tbsp chopped fresh parsley
- 2 tbsp chopped fresh thyme
- 2 cloves garlic, minced
- 1 lemon, zest and juice
- Salt and pepper to taste
- 1 tbsp balsamic vinegar

Directions:

1. Preheat the oven to 400°F (200°C).
2. In a bowl, combine olive oil, chopped parsley, chopped thyme, minced garlic, lemon zest, lemon juice, salt, and pepper.
3. Place the chicken breasts on a baking sheet lined with parchment paper.
4. Spread the herb mixture evenly over each chicken breast, ensuring they are thoroughly coated.
5. Drizzle balsamic vinegar over the chicken breasts.
6. Roast in the preheated oven for approximately 20-25 minutes or until the chicken reaches an internal temperature of 165°F (74°C) and the juices run clear.
7. Allow the Herb-Roasted Chicken Breasts to rest for a few minutes before serving.

Useful Tip: For extra tenderness, marinate the chicken breasts in the herb mixture for 30 minutes before roasting.

Nutritional values: Calories: 220 kcal | Fat: 10 g | Protein: 30 g | Carbs: 2 g | Net carbs: 1 g | Fiber: 1 g | Cholesterol: 80 mg | Sodium: 90 mg | Potassium: 550 mg

LEMON GARLIC GRILLED TURKEY CUTLETS

Serving: 4 | Prep time: 15 minutes | Cook time: 10 minutes

Ingredients:

- 4 turkey cutlets (4 oz / 113 g each)
- 2 tbsp olive oil
- Zest and juice of 1 lemon
- 2 cloves garlic, minced
- 1 tbsp chopped fresh parsley
- Salt and pepper to taste
- 1 tbsp balsamic vinegar

Directions:

1. Preheat the grill to medium-high heat.

2. In a bowl, mix together olive oil, lemon zest, lemon juice, minced garlic, chopped parsley, salt, and pepper.

3. Brush the turkey cutlets with the lemon garlic marinade.

4. Place the marinated turkey cutlets on the preheated grill.

5. Grill for approximately 4-5 minutes on each side or until the turkey is cooked through and reaches an internal temperature of 165°F (74°C).

6. Drizzle balsamic vinegar over the grilled turkey cutlets just before removing them from the grill.

Useful Tip: Marinate the turkey cutlets for 30 minutes before grilling to enhance the flavor.

Nutritional values: Calories: 220 kcal | Fat: 10 g | Protein: 30 g | Carbs: 2 g | Net carbs: 1 g |
Fiber: 1 g | Cholesterol: 80 mg | Sodium: 90 mg | Potassium: 550 mg

ROSEMARY BAKED CHICKEN THIGHS

Serving: 4 | Prep time: 10 minutes | Cook time: 25 minutes

Ingredients:

- 4 chicken thighs (4 oz / 113 g each), bone-in, skinless
- 2 tbsp olive oil
- 2 cloves garlic, minced
- 1 tbsp chopped fresh rosemary
- Zest of 1 lemon
- Salt and pepper to taste
- 1 tbsp lemon juice
- 1 tsp honey

Directions:

1. Preheat the oven to 400°F (200°C).

2. In a bowl, combine olive oil, minced garlic, chopped rosemary, lemon zest, salt, and pepper.

3. Rub the chicken thighs with this herb mixture, ensuring they are well coated.

4. Place the chicken thighs in a baking dish and bake for 20-25 minutes or until the chicken reaches an internal temperature of 165°F (74°C).

5. In a small bowl, mix lemon juice and honey.

6. Brush the lemon-honey mixture over the baked chicken thighs during the last 5 minutes of baking.

Useful Tip: For a crispy texture, broil the chicken thighs for an additional 2-3 minutes after brushing them with the lemon-honey mixture.

Nutritional values: Calories: 250 kcal | Fat: 15 g | Protein: 24 g | Carbs: 2 g | Net carbs: 1 g |
Fiber: 1 g | Cholesterol: 110 mg | Sodium: 90 mg | Potassium: 270 mg

TURKEY AND VEGETABLE SKEWERS

Serving: 4 | Prep time: 15 minutes | Cook time: 15 minutes

Ingredients:

- 16 oz (450 g) turkey breast, cut into cubes
- 1 zucchini, sliced into rounds
- 1 red bell pepper, cut into chunks
- 1 yellow bell pepper, cut into chunks
- 1 red onion, cut into wedges
- 2 tbsp olive oil, salt
- 2 tbsp chopped fresh parsley
- 1 tbsp lemon juice

Directions:

1. Preheat the grill to medium-high heat (about 375°F/190°C).
2. Thread the turkey, zucchini, bell peppers, and red onion onto skewers, alternating between ingredients.
3. In a bowl, mix olive oil, chopped parsley, salt and lemon juice.
4. Brush the skewers with this herb mixture.
5. Grill the skewers for 12-15 minutes, turning occasionally, until the turkey is cooked through and the vegetables are tender.

Useful Tip: Soak wooden skewers in water for 30 minutes before grilling to prevent burning.

Nutritional values: Calories: 280 kcal | Fat: 12 g | Protein: 30 g | Carbs: 10 g | Net carbs: 8 g | Fiber: 2 g | Cholesterol: 70 mg | Sodium: 80 mg | Potassium: 650 mg

LEMON HERB GRILLED CHICKEN SKEWERS

Serving: 4 | Prep time: 20 minutes | Cook time: 15 minutes

Ingredients:

- 16 oz (450 g) chicken breast, cut into cubes
- 1 zucchini, sliced into rounds
- 1 yellow bell pepper, cut into chunks
- 1 red onion, cut into wedges
- 2 tbsp olive oil, salt
- 2 cloves garlic, minced
- 1 tbsp lemon juice
- 1 tbsp chopped fresh thyme

Directions:

1. Preheat the grill to medium-high heat (about 375°F/190°C).
2. Thread the chicken, zucchini, bell pepper, and red onion onto skewers, alternating between pieces.
3. In a bowl, mix olive oil, minced garlic, lemon juice, salt and chopped thyme.
4. Brush the skewers generously with this herb mixture.
5. Grill the skewers for 12-15 minutes, turning occasionally, until the chicken is thoroughly cooked.

Useful Tip: Soak wooden skewers in water for 30 minutes before grilling to prevent burning.

Nutritional values: Calories: 280 kcal | Fat: 12 g | Protein: 30 g | Carbs: 8 g | Net carbs: 6 g | Fiber: 2 g | Cholesterol: 70 mg | Sodium: 80 mg | Potassium: 650 mg

TURKEY AND SPINACH MEATBALLS

Serving: 4 | Prep time: 15 minutes | Cook time: 20 minutes

Ingredients:

- 16 oz (450 g) ground turkey
- 4 oz (113 g) fresh spinach, finely chopped
- 1/2 onion, finely chopped
- 2 cloves garlic, minced
- 1 oz (25 g) almond flour
- 1 egg
- 1 tbsp olive oil
- Salt and pepper to taste

Directions:

1. Preheat the oven to 375°F (190°C).
2. In a bowl, combine ground turkey, chopped spinach, onion, garlic, almond flour, egg, salt, and pepper.
3. Mix thoroughly until well combined.
4. Shape the mixture into meatballs of equal size.
5. Heat olive oil in an ovenproof skillet over medium heat.
6. Brown the meatballs on all sides for about 5 minutes.
7. Transfer the skillet to the preheated oven and bake for 12-15 minutes until cooked through.

Useful Tip: For extra moisture and tenderness, add a tablespoon of unsweetened applesauce to the meatball mixture.

Nutritional values: Calories: 240 kcal | Fat: 15 g | Protein: 25 g | Carbs: 4 g | Net carbs: 2 g | Fiber: 2 g | Cholesterol: 90 mg | Sodium: 70 mg | Potassium: 400 mg

ITALIAN HERB BAKED CHICKEN DRUMSTICKS

Serving: 4 | Prep time: 10 minutes | Cook time: 35 minutes

Ingredients:

- 8 chicken drumsticks (approx. 32 oz / 900 g)
- 2 tbsp olive oil
- 2 cloves garlic, minced
- 1 tbsp lemon juice
- 1 tsp dried oregano
- 1 tsp dried basil
- 1/2 tsp dried thyme
- Salt and pepper to taste

Directions:

1. Preheat the oven to 400°F (200°C).
2. In a bowl, combine olive oil, minced garlic, lemon juice, dried oregano, dried basil, dried thyme, salt, and pepper.
3. Pat dry the chicken drumsticks with paper towels.
4. Brush the drumsticks generously with the herb mixture.

5. Place the drumsticks on a baking sheet lined with parchment paper.

6. Bake in the preheated oven for 30-35 minutes until golden brown and cooked through, turning them halfway through.

Useful Tip: For extra tenderness, marinate the drumsticks in the herb mixture for 30 minutes before baking.

Nutritional values: Calories: 280 kcal | Fat: 16 g | Protein: 30 g | Carbs: 1 g | Net carbs: 0 g | Fiber: 1 g | Cholesterol: 120 mg | Sodium: 110 mg | Potassium: 350 mg

LEMON THYME GRILLED TURKEY BREAST

Serving: 4 | Prep time: 10 minutes | Cook time: 20 minutes

Ingredients:

- 24 oz (680 g) turkey breast, boneless and skinless
- 2 tbsp olive oil
- Zest of 1 lemon
- Juice of 1 lemon
- 2 tsp fresh thyme leaves
- 2 cloves garlic, minced
- Salt and pepper to taste

Directions:

1. Preheat the grill to medium-high heat.

2. In a bowl, mix together olive oil, lemon zest, lemon juice, fresh thyme leaves, minced garlic, salt, and pepper.

3. Pat dry the turkey breast with paper towels.

4. Brush the turkey breast generously with the lemon-thyme mixture.

5. Grill the turkey breast for about 8-10 minutes per side, until the internal temperature reaches 165°F (74°C) and the juices run clear.

Useful Tip: Let the turkey breast rest for 5-10 minutes after grilling before slicing to keep the juices intact and ensure tenderness.

Nutritional values: Calories: 180 kcal | Fat: 5 g | Protein: 30 g | Carbs: 1 g | Net carbs: 0 g | Fiber: 0 g | Cholesterol: 80 mg | Sodium: 80 mg | Potassium: 320 mg

HERBED CHICKEN AND VEGGIE FOIL PACKETS

Serving: 4 | Prep time: 15 minutes | Cook time: 25 minutes

Ingredients:

- 24 oz (680 g) chicken breasts, boneless and skinless, cut into chunks
- 2 medium zucchinis, sliced
- 2 red bell peppers, sliced
- 1 large onion, sliced
- 2 tbsp olive oil
- 2 cloves garlic, minced
- 1 tsp dried oregano
- Salt and pepper to taste

Directions:

1. Preheat the oven to 400°F (200°C).
2. In a bowl, combine the chicken chunks, zucchini slices, red bell pepper slices, onion slices, minced garlic, olive oil, dried oregano, salt, and pepper. Toss until well coated.
3. Lay out four large pieces of aluminum foil. Divide the chicken and veggie mixture equally among the foil pieces.
4. Fold the foil over the ingredients and seal the edges to create packets.
5. Place the packets on a baking sheet and bake for 20-25 minutes until the chicken is cooked through and the veggies are tender.

Useful Tip: Feel free to customize by adding your choice of herbs or a squeeze of lemon for a zesty touch before sealing the packets.

Nutritional values: Calories: 280 kcal | Fat: 10 g | Protein: 35 g | Carbs: 10 g | Net carbs: 8 g | Fiber: 2 g | Cholesterol: 90 mg | Sodium: 80 mg | Potassium: 820 mg

TURKEY AND QUINOA STUFFED PEPPERS

Serving: 4 | Prep time: 20 minutes | Cook time: 40 minutes

Ingredients:

- 4 large bell peppers, halved and seeds removed
- 16 oz (454 g) ground turkey
- 5 oz (185 g) cooked quinoa
- 5 oz (150 g) diced tomatoes
- 2 oz (75 g) chopped onion
- 2 cloves garlic, minced
- 1 tsp dried Italian seasoning
- 2 tbsp olive oil
- Salt and pepper to taste

Directions:

1. Preheat the oven to 375°F (190°C).
2. In a skillet over medium heat, warm the olive oil. Add the onion and garlic, sauté until fragrant, about 2 minutes.
3. Add the ground turkey to the skillet, breaking it apart as it cooks until browned.

4. Stir in the diced tomatoes, cooked quinoa, dried Italian seasoning, salt, and pepper. Cook for an additional 5 minutes, allowing the flavors to blend.

5. Fill each bell pepper half with the turkey and quinoa mixture.

6. Place the stuffed peppers on a baking dish, cover with foil, and bake for 25-30 minutes until the peppers are tender.

Useful Tip: Experiment with different colored bell peppers for a vibrant presentation and varied nutrient profiles.

Nutritional values: Calories: 320 kcal | Fat: 14 g | Protein: 25 g | Carbs: 24 g | Net carbs: 18 g | Fiber: 6 g | Cholesterol: 65 mg | Sodium: 130 mg | Potassium: 860 mg

RABBIT AND VEGETABLE SKEWERS

Serving: 4 | Prep time: 20 minutes | Cook time: 15 minutes

Ingredients:

- 16 oz (454 g) rabbit meat, cut into chunks
- 1 bell pepper, cut into squares
- 1 zucchini, sliced into rounds
- 1 red onion, cut into wedges
- 8 cherry tomatoes
- 2 tbsp olive oil
- 2 cloves garlic, minced
- 1 tsp dried thyme
- Salt and pepper to taste

Directions:

1. Preheat the grill to medium-high heat (around 400°F/200°C).

2. In a bowl, combine the olive oil, minced garlic, dried thyme, salt, and pepper.

3. Thread the rabbit chunks, bell pepper, zucchini, red onion, and cherry tomatoes onto skewers, alternating the ingredients.

4. Brush the skewers generously with the olive oil mixture.

5. Place the skewers on the grill and cook for about 10-12 minutes, turning occasionally until the rabbit is cooked through and the vegetables are slightly charred.

6. Remove from the grill and let them rest for a couple of minutes before serving.

Useful Tip: Soak wooden skewers in water for about 30 minutes before grilling to prevent them from burning.

Nutritional values: Calories: 240 kcal | Fat: 12 g | Protein: 28 g | Carbs: 8 g | Net carbs: 5 g | Fiber: 3 g | Cholesterol: 80 mg | Sodium: 65 mg | Potassium: 890 mg

HERBED RABBIT STEW

Serving: 4 | Prep time: 15 minutes | Cook time: 45 minutes

Ingredients:

- 20 oz (567 g) rabbit meat, cut into pieces
- 2 tbsp olive oil
- 2 carrots, chopped
- 1 onion, diced
- 2 cloves garlic, minced
- 16 oz (480 ml) low-sodium chicken broth
- 1 tbsp tomato paste
- 1 tsp dried thyme
- Salt and pepper to taste

Directions:

1. In a large pot over medium heat, warm the olive oil.
2. Add the rabbit pieces and brown them on all sides for about 5-7 minutes.
3. Stir in the diced onion, minced garlic, and chopped carrots, cooking for an additional 3-4 minutes until slightly softened.
4. Add the low-sodium chicken broth, tomato paste, dried thyme, salt, and pepper, stirring well.
5. Bring the mixture to a boil, then reduce the heat to low, cover the pot, and let it simmer for about 35-40 minutes or until the rabbit is tender and cooked through.
6. Serve the herbed rabbit stew hot, garnished with fresh herbs if desired.

Useful Tip: To add extra richness, consider adding a splash of white wine when adding the broth.

Nutritional values: Calories: 250 kcal | Fat: 10 g | Protein: 30 g | Carbs: 8 g | Net carbs: 5 g | Fiber: 3 g | Cholesterol: 90 mg | Sodium: 380 mg | Potassium: 760 mg

RABBIT AND MUSHROOM SAUTÉ

Serving: 4 | Prep time: 10 minutes | Cook time: 20 minutes

Ingredients:

- 16 oz (454 g) rabbit meat, diced
- 8 oz (227 g) mushrooms, sliced
- 2 tbsp olive oil
- 2 cloves garlic, minced
- 1 onion, finely chopped
- 4 oz (120 ml) low-sodium chicken broth
- 1 tsp dried thyme
- Salt and pepper to taste

Directions:

1. Heat olive oil in a skillet over medium heat.
2. Add diced rabbit meat and cook until it browns, about 5-7 minutes.
3. Stir in the minced garlic and chopped onion, sautéing until fragrant and onions turn translucent.
4. Add the sliced mushrooms, cooking for an additional 3-4 minutes until they soften.
5. Pour in the low-sodium chicken broth, sprinkle with dried thyme, salt, and pepper, stirring well.

6. Reduce heat to low, cover the skillet, and let it simmer for 8-10 minutes or until the rabbit is tender and cooked through.

7. Serve the Rabbit and Mushroom Sauté hot.

Useful Tip: For added richness, finish the dish with a splash of white wine before simmering.

Nutritional values: Calories: 220 kcal | Fat: 12 g | Protein: 25 g | Carbs: 5 g | Net carbs: 4 g | Fiber: 1 g | Cholesterol: 80 mg | Sodium: 230 mg | Potassium: 640 mg

BRAISED RABBIT WITH ROOT VEGETABLES

Serving: 4 | Prep time: 15 minutes | Cook time: 45 minutes

Ingredients:

- 16 oz (454 g) rabbit meat, cut into pieces
- 4 oz (113 g) carrots, sliced
- 4 oz (113 g) parsnips, chopped
- 4 oz (113 g) turnips, diced
- 2 tbsp olive oil
- 2 cloves garlic, minced
- 16 oz (480 ml) low-sodium chicken broth
- 1 tbsp balsamic vinegar
- Salt and pepper to taste

Directions:

1. Heat olive oil in a large skillet or Dutch oven over medium heat.

2. Brown the rabbit pieces for 3-4 minutes per side.

3. Add minced garlic, sliced carrots, chopped parsnips, and diced turnips, sautéing for an additional 5 minutes.

4. Pour in low-sodium chicken broth and balsamic vinegar, season with salt and pepper, and bring to a gentle boil.

5. Reduce heat to low, cover, and simmer for 30-35 minutes or until the rabbit is tender and the vegetables are cooked through.

6. Serve the Braised Rabbit with Root Vegetables hot.

Useful Tip: For an extra depth of flavor, consider adding a sprig of fresh rosemary or thyme during simmering.

Nutritional values: Calories: 280 kcal | Fat: 12 g | Protein: 32 g | Carbs: 10 g | Net carbs: 7 g | Fiber: 3 g | Cholesterol: 90 mg | Sodium: 330 mg | Potassium: 750 mg

ROSEMARY GARLIC GRILLED RABBIT

Serving: 4 | Prep time: 20 minutes | Cook time: 20 minutes

Ingredients:

- 20 oz (567 g) rabbit meat, cut into pieces
- 2 tbsp olive oil
- 2 cloves garlic, minced
- 1 tbsp fresh rosemary, chopped
- 1 tbsp lemon juice
- 1/2 tsp lemon zest
- Salt and pepper to taste

Directions:

1. Preheat your grill to medium-high heat (around 375°F/190°C).

2. In a bowl, mix together olive oil, minced garlic, chopped rosemary, lemon juice, lemon zest, salt, and pepper.

3. Coat the rabbit pieces evenly with this mixture and let it marinate for at least 10 minutes.

4. Place the rabbit pieces on the grill and cook for about 8-10 minutes per side or until they reach an internal temperature of 160°F (71°C).

5. Remove from the grill and let the rabbit rest for a few minutes before serving.

Useful Tip: To prevent the rabbit from drying out, brush it with the marinade during grilling to keep it moist and flavorful.

Nutritional values: Calories: 280 kcal | Fat: 14 g | Protein: 36 g | Carbs: 2 g | Net carbs: 1 g | Fiber: 1 g | Cholesterol: 120 mg | Sodium: 75 mg | Potassium: 450 mg

VEGAN RECIPES

LENTIL AND VEGETABLE STEW

Serving: 4 | Prep time: 15 minutes | Cook time: 30 minutes

Ingredients:

- 8 oz (227 g) lentils
- 1 medium onion, chopped
- 2 cloves garlic, minced
- 2 carrots, diced
- 2 celery stalks, chopped
- 1 can (14 oz / 400 g) diced tomatoes
- 33 oz (946 ml) vegetable broth
- 1 tbsp olive oil
- Salt and pepper to taste

Directions:

1. Heat olive oil in a pot over medium heat, add onion and garlic, and sauté until fragrant.
2. Add carrots, celery, lentils, diced tomatoes, and vegetable broth, bring to a boil.
3. Reduce heat, cover, and simmer for 25-30 minutes until lentils and vegetables are tender.
4. Season with salt and pepper to taste.

Useful Tip: For added flavor, toss in a sprig of fresh thyme or a pinch of smoked paprika.

Nutritional values: Calories: 250 kcal | Fat: 3 g | Protein: 16 g | Carbs: 45 g | Net carbs: 35 g | Fiber: 10 g | Cholesterol: 0 mg | Sodium: 700 mg | Potassium: 800 mg

QUINOA AND ROASTED VEGGIE BOWL

Serving: 4 | Prep time: 20 minutes | Cook time: 25 minutes

Ingredients:

- 8 oz (227 g) quinoa, cooked
- 1 bell pepper, diced
- 1 zucchini, sliced
- 5 oz (150 g) cherry tomatoes
- 5 oz (150 g) broccoli florets
- 2 tbsp olive oil
- 1 tsp dried oregano
- 1 tsp garlic powder
- Salt and pepper to taste

Directions:

1. Preheat oven to 400°F (200°C). Toss bell pepper, zucchini, cherry tomatoes, and broccoli with olive oil, oregano, salt, pepper and garlic powder.
2. Spread vegetables on a baking sheet and roast for 20-25 minutes until lightly browned.
3. Divide cooked quinoa among bowls and top with roasted vegetables.

Useful Tip: Drizzle with a squeeze of lemon juice for an extra zesty touch.

Nutritional values: Calories: 320 kcal | Fat: 12 g | Protein: 10 g | Carbs: 45 g | Net carbs: 35 g | Fiber: 10 g | Cholesterol: 0 mg | Sodium: 30 mg | Potassium: 600 mg

CHICKPEA AND SPINACH CURRY

Serving: 4 | **Prep time:** 15 minutes | **Cook time:** 25 minutes

Ingredients:

- 16 oz (454 g) canned chickpeas, drained
- 1 onion, finely chopped
- 2 cloves garlic, minced
- 2 tsp curry powder
- 1 can (14 oz / 400 ml) coconut milk
- 33 oz (946 ml) fresh spinach
- 2 tbsp olive oil
- Salt and pepper to taste

Directions:

1. Heat olive oil in a pan, sauté onion and garlic until softened.
2. Add curry powder, chickpeas, salt, pepper and coconut milk, simmer for 15 minutes.
3. Add fresh spinach, cook for an additional 5 minutes until wilted.
4. Serve over brown rice or quinoa.

Useful Tip: Garnish with chopped cilantro or a dollop of dairy-free yogurt.

Nutritional values: Calories: 320 kcal | Fat: 20 g | Protein: 10 g | Carbs: 30 g | Net carbs: 20 g | Fiber: 10 g | Cholesterol: 0 mg | Sodium: 300 mg | Potassium: 700 mg

TOFU STIR-FRY WITH BROCCOLI AND BELL PEPPERS

Serving: 4 | **Prep time:** 15 minutes | **Cook time:** 15 minutes

Ingredients:

- 14 oz (397 g) firm tofu, cubed
- 5 oz (150 g) broccoli florets
- 2 bell peppers, sliced
- 2 tbsp sesame oil
- 2 cloves garlic, minced
- 2 tbsp low-sodium soy sauce
- 1 tsp rice vinegar

Directions:

1. Heat sesame oil in a pan, add minced garlic, and cook until fragrant.
2. Add tofu cubes and sauté until lightly golden.
3. Stir in broccoli and bell peppers, cook for 5-7 minutes until vegetables are tender-crisp.
4. Drizzle with soy sauce and rice vinegar, toss to coat evenly.

Useful Tip: For added depth, sprinkle toasted sesame seeds on top before serving.

Nutritional values: Calories: 260 kcal | Fat: 15 g | Protein: 18 g | Carbs: 15 g | Net carbs: 10 g | Fiber: 5 g | Cholesterol: 0 mg | Sodium: 450 mg | Potassium: 650 mg

ROASTED CAULIFLOWER STEAKS WITH HERBED DRESSING

Serving: 4 | Prep time: 10 minutes | Cook time: 25 minutes

Ingredients:

- 1 head cauliflower, sliced into steaks
- 4 tbsp olive oil
- 2 tbsp balsamic vinegar
- 1 tsp dried thyme
- Salt and pepper to taste

Directions:

1. Preheat oven to 400°F (200°C). Place cauliflower steaks on a baking sheet.
2. Whisk together olive oil, balsamic vinegar, dried thyme, salt, and pepper.
3. Brush the mixture onto cauliflower steaks, roast for 20-25 minutes until golden and tender.

Useful Tip: Garnish with a squeeze of lemon juice and fresh parsley for a burst of flavor.

Nutritional values: Calories: 180 kcal | Fat: 14 g | Protein: 5 g | Carbs: 10 g | Net carbs: 5 g | Fiber: 5 g | Cholesterol: 0 mg | Sodium: 50 mg | Potassium: 600 mg

SWEET POTATO AND BLACK BEAN TACOS

Serving: 4 | Prep time: 20 minutes | Cook time: 20 minutes

Ingredients:

- 2 large sweet potatoes, diced
- 15 oz (425 g) canned black beans, drained
- 8 small corn tortillas
- 1 avocado, sliced
- 1 lime, juiced
- 2 tbsp olive oil

Directions:

1. Roast diced sweet potatoes in olive oil at 400°F (200°C) for 20 minutes until tender.
2. Warm corn tortillas in a skillet.
3. Fill tortillas with roasted sweet potatoes, black beans, and sliced avocado.
4. Squeeze lime juice over the tacos before serving.

Useful Tip: Top with a dollop of dairy-free yogurt and fresh cilantro for extra creaminess and flavor.

Nutritional values: Calories: 280 kcal | Fat: 10 g | Protein: 8 g | Carbs: 40 g | Net carbs: 30 g | Fiber: 10 g | Cholesterol: 0 mg | Sodium: 150 mg | Potassium: 750 mg

ZUCCHINI NOODLES WITH TOMATO BASIL SAUCE

Serving: 4 | Prep time: 15 minutes | Cook time: 10 minutes

Ingredients:

- 4 medium zucchinis, spiralized
- 17 oz (500 ml) tomato sauce
- 1 oz (30 g) fresh basil leaves
- 2 tbsp olive oil
- 2 cloves garlic, minced
- 1 oz (30 g) pine nuts
- Nutritional yeast for garnish
- Salt and pepper to taste

Directions:

1. Heat olive oil in a pan, add minced garlic, and lightly toast the pine nuts.
2. Pour in the tomato sauce, salt, pepper and bring to a gentle simmer.
3. Add zucchini noodles and cook for 3-4 minutes until tender.
4. Toss in fresh basil leaves and serve topped with nutritional yeast.

Useful Tip: For added protein, sprinkle hemp seeds or add cooked lentils to the sauce.

Nutritional values: Calories: 220 kcal | Fat: 15 g | Protein: 5 g | Carbs: 20 g | Net carbs: 15 g | Fiber: 5 g | Cholesterol: 0 mg | Sodium: 400 mg | Potassium: 800 mg

MUSHROOM AND SPINACH RISOTTO

Serving: 4 | Prep time: 10 minutes | Cook time: 30 minutes

Ingredients:

- 15 oz (400 g) Arborio rice
- 33 oz (1 liter) vegetable broth
- 8 oz (227 g) mushrooms, sliced
- 2 oz (60 g) spinach leaves
- 2 tbsp olive oil
- 2 cloves garlic, minced
- 0,5 oz (15 g) nutritional yeast
- Salt and pepper to taste

Directions:

1. Sauté minced garlic in olive oil, add sliced mushrooms, and cook until tender.
2. Stir in Arborio rice , salt, pepper and cook for a minute.
3. Gradually add vegetable broth, one cup at a time, stirring constantly until absorbed.
4. Fold in spinach leaves and nutritional yeast before serving.

Useful Tip: Substitute some of the broth with unsweetened almond milk for a creamier texture.

Nutritional values: Calories: 280 kcal | Fat: 10 g | Protein: 8 g | Carbs: 40 g | Net carbs: 30 g | Fiber: 10 g | Cholesterol: 0 mg | Sodium: 900 mg | Potassium: 600 mg

VEGAN VEGETABLE STIR-FRIED RICE

Serving: 4 | Prep time: 15 minutes | Cook time: 15 minutes

Ingredients:

- 14 oz (400 g) cooked brown rice
- 5 oz (150 g) mixed vegetables (peas, carrots, bell peppers)
- 5 oz (150 g) broccoli florets
- 2 tbsp low-sodium soy sauce
- 2 tbsp sesame oil
- 1 tsp rice vinegar
- 0,5 oz (15 g) chopped green onions
- Salt and pepper to taste

Directions:

1. Heat sesame oil in a wok, add mixed vegetables and broccoli, stir-fry until tender.
2. Add cooked brown rice, soy sauce, salt, pepper and rice vinegar, toss until well combined.
3. Garnish with chopped green onions before serving.

Useful Tip: Use tamari for a gluten-free alternative to soy sauce.

Nutritional values: Calories: 240 kcal | Fat: 8 g | Protein: 6 g | Carbs: 35 g | Net carbs: 25 g | Fiber: 10 g | Cholesterol: 0 mg | Sodium: 500 mg | Potassium: 400 mg

STUFFED BELL PEPPERS WITH BROWN RICE AND VEGGIES

Serving: 4 | Prep time: 20 minutes | Cook time: 30 minutes

Ingredients:

- 4 bell peppers, halved and deseeded
- 14 oz (400 g) cooked brown rice
- 5 oz (150 g) mixed vegetables (corn, peas, carrots)
- 5 oz (150 g) diced tomatoes
- 0,5 oz (15 g) chopped parsley
- Salt and pepper to taste

Directions:

1. Preheat oven to 375°F (190°C). Parboil bell peppers in boiling water for 2-3 minutes, then drain.
2. In a bowl, mix cooked brown rice, mixed vegetables, diced tomatoes, chopped parsley, salt, and pepper.
3. Stuff bell pepper halves with the mixture and bake for 25-30 minutes until peppers are tender.

Useful Tip: Top with a sprinkle of nutritional yeast for added flavor.

Nutritional values: Calories: 200 kcal | Fat: 6 g | Protein: 5 g | Carbs: 30 g | Net carbs: 20 g | Fiber: 10 g | Cholesterol: 0 mg | Sodium: 300 mg | Potassium: 600 mg

HEARTY VEGETABLE AND LENTIL SOUP

Serving: 4 | Prep time: 15 minutes | Cook time: 30 minutes

Ingredients:

- 7 oz (200 g) lentils
- 33 oz (1 liter) vegetable broth
- 2 carrots, diced
- 2 celery stalks, chopped
- 1 onion, diced
- 2 cloves garlic, minced
- 7 oz (200 g) spinach leaves
- 2 tbsp olive oil
- Salt and pepper to taste

Directions:

1. In a pot, heat olive oil, sauté onion and garlic until fragrant.
2. Add carrots, celery, lentils, salt, pepper and vegetable broth, bring to a boil.
3. Simmer for 20-25 minutes until lentils are tender.
4. Stir in spinach leaves, cook for another 5 minutes.
5. Serve warm.

Useful Tip: Blend half of the soup for a thicker texture.

Nutritional values: Calories: 280 kcal | Fat: 8 g | Protein: 15 g | Carbs: 40 g | Net carbs: 30 g | Fiber: 15 g | Cholesterol: 0 mg | Sodium: 900 mg | Potassium: 1200 mg

CREAMY CAULIFLOWER AND BROCCOLI SOUP

Serving: 4 | Prep time: 10 minutes | Cook time: 25 minutes

Ingredients:

- 1 head cauliflower, chopped
- 7 oz (200 g) broccoli florets
- 33 oz (1 liter) vegetable broth
- 1 onion, chopped
- 2 cloves garlic, minced
- 4 oz (120 ml) unsweetened almond milk
- 2 tbsp olive oil
- Salt and pepper to taste

Directions:

1. Sauté onion and garlic in olive oil until softened.
2. Add cauliflower, broccoli, , salt, pepper and vegetable broth. Simmer for 20 minutes until veggies are tender.
3. Blend the mixture until smooth, return to the pot.
4. Stir in almond milk, simmer for 5 more minutes.
5. Serve hot.

TOMATO BASIL QUINOA SOUP

Serving: 4 | Prep time: 10 minutes | Cook time: 25 minutes

Ingredients:

- 6 oz (185 g) quinoa, rinsed
- 33 oz (1 liter) low-sodium vegetable broth
- 14 oz (400 g) diced tomatoes
- 2 oz (30 g) fresh basil leaves
- 2 tbsp olive oil
- 2 cloves garlic, minced
- Salt and pepper to taste

Directions:

1. Heat olive oil, sauté garlic until golden.
2. Add quinoa, vegetable broth, and diced tomatoes, simmer for 20 minutes until quinoa is cooked.
3. Stir in fresh basil leaves, cook for an additional 5 minutes.
4. Season with salt and pepper.
5. Serve warm.

Useful Tip: Garnish with a drizzle of extra-virgin olive oil for enhanced flavor.

Nutritional values: Calories: 260 kcal | Fat: 8 g | Protein: 10 g | Carbs: 40 g | Net carbs: 30 g | Fiber: 5 g | Cholesterol: 0 mg | Sodium: 1000 mg | Potassium: 800 mg

SPINACH AND WHITE BEAN SOUP

Serving: 4 | Prep time: 15 minutes | Cook time: 25 minutes

Ingredients:

- 1 can (15 oz / 425 g) white beans, drained and rinsed
- 33 oz (1 liter) low-sodium vegetable broth
- 1 onion, finely chopped
- 2 cloves garlic, minced
- 4 oz (120 g) fresh spinach leaves
- 1 tbsp olive oil
- 1 bay leaf
- Salt and pepper to taste

Directions:

1. Heat olive oil in a pot, sauté onions until translucent, then add minced garlic and cook for another minute.
2. Pour in the vegetable broth, salt, pepper and bring to a simmer, then add the white beans and bay leaf.

3. Simmer for 15 minutes, add fresh spinach leaves, and cook for an additional 5 minutes until wilted.

Useful Tip: Enhance the flavor by sprinkling some grated Parmesan cheese before serving.

Nutritional values: Calories: 180 kcal | Fat: 4 g | Protein: 8 g | Carbs: 30 g | Net carbs: 20 g | Fiber: 10 g | Cholesterol: 0 mg | Sodium: 700 mg | Potassium: 800 mg

BUTTERNUT SQUASH AND APPLE SOUP

Serving: 4 | Prep time: 20 minutes | Cook time: 30 minutes

Ingredients:

- 1 medium butternut squash, peeled and diced
- 2 apples, peeled, cored, and chopped
- 33 oz (1 liter) low-sodium vegetable broth
- 1 onion, diced
- 2 tbsp olive oil
- 1/2 tsp ground cinnamon
- Salt and pepper to taste

Directions:

1. In a pot, heat olive oil and sauté onions until soft, then add diced butternut squash and chopped apples.

2. Add vegetable broth and bring to a boil, reduce heat, cover, and simmer for 20-25 minutes until squash is tender.

3. Blend the soup until smooth, season with ground cinnamon, salt, pepper, and simmer for an additional 5 minutes.

Useful Tip: Garnish with a dollop of Greek yogurt for added creaminess and a touch of tang.

Nutritional values: Calories: 220 kcal | Fat: 7 g | Protein: 5 g | Carbs: 40 g | Net carbs: 30 g | Fiber: 10 g | Cholesterol: 0 mg | Sodium: 600 mg | Potassium: 1000 mg

BERRY BLAST GREEN SMOOTHIE

Serving: 4 | Prep time: 10 minutes | Cook time: 0 minutes

Ingredients:

- 9 oz (280 g) mixed berries (strawberries, blueberries, raspberries)
- 2.1 oz (60 g) fresh spinach leaves
- 1 banana, peeled
- 8 oz (240 ml) unsweetened almond milk
- 4 oz (120 g) Greek yogurt
- 1 tbsp chia seeds

Directions:

1. Combine all ingredients in a blender.
2. Blend until smooth and creamy.
3. Add more almond milk if a thinner consistency is desired.

Useful Tip: Boost the protein content by adding a scoop of plant-based protein powder.

Nutritional values: Calories: 120 kcal | Fat: 3 g | Protein: 6 g | Carbs: 20 g | Net carbs: 14 g | Fiber: 6 g | Cholesterol: 0 mg | Sodium: 90 mg | Potassium: 380 mg

MANGO PINEAPPLE TURMERIC SMOOTHIE

Serving: 4 | Prep time: 10 minutes | Cook time: 0 minutes

Ingredients:

- 9.5 oz (300 g) mango chunks
- 10.5 oz (300 g) pineapple chunks
- 1 banana, peeled
- 1/2 tsp ground turmeric
- 8 oz (240 ml) coconut water
- 1 tbsp flaxseeds

Directions:

1. Place all ingredients into a blender.
2. Blend until smooth.
3. Adjust the consistency with more coconut water if needed.

Useful Tip: Add a handful of kale for an extra nutrient boost without altering the flavor significantly.

Nutritional values: Calories: 160 kcal | Fat: 2 g | Protein: 3 g | Carbs: 36 g | Net carbs: 28 g | Fiber: 8 g | Cholesterol: 0 mg | Sodium: 50 mg | Potassium: 650 mg

SPINACH BANANA ALMOND SMOOTHIE

Serving: 4 | Prep time: 5 minutes | Cook time: 0 minutes

Ingredients:

- 6 oz (170 g) fresh spinach leaves
- 2 ripe bananas, peeled
- 4 tbsp almond butter
- 16 oz (480 ml) unsweetened almond milk
- 2 tbsp chia seeds

Directions:

1. Blend spinach and almond milk until smooth.

2. Add bananas, almond butter, and chia seeds.

3. Blend until creamy and well combined.

Useful Tip: Enhance the creaminess by using frozen bananas.

Nutritional values: Calories: 230 kcal | Fat: 14 g | Protein: 7 g | Carbs: 23 g | Net carbs: 12 g | Fiber: 11 g | Cholesterol: 0 mg | Sodium: 180 mg | Potassium: 610 mg

BLUEBERRY KALE PROTEIN SMOOTHIE

Serving: 4 | Prep time: 5 minutes | Cook time: 0 minutes

Ingredients:

- 8 oz (227 g) kale leaves
- 10 oz (280 g) blueberries (fresh or frozen)
- 4 oz (120 ml) unsweetened Greek yogurt
- 16 oz (480 ml) coconut water
- 2 tbsp hemp seeds

Directions:

1. Blend kale and coconut water until smooth.

2. Add blueberries, Greek yogurt, and hemp seeds.

3. Blend until all ingredients are well combined.

Useful Tip: For added sweetness, consider including a ripe banana.

Nutritional values: Calories: 180 kcal | Fat: 5 g | Protein: 8 g | Carbs: 27 g | Net carbs: 19 g | Fiber: 8 g | Cholesterol: 0 mg | Sodium: 100 mg | Potassium: 680 mg

CITRUS CARROT GINGER SMOOTHIE

Serving: 4 | Prep time: 5 minutes | Cook time: 0 minutes

Ingredients:

- 12 oz (340 g) carrots, peeled and chopped
- Juice of 3 oranges
- 1 tsp freshly grated ginger
- 1 tsp honey (optional for sweetness)
- 12 oz (360 ml) coconut water
- 1 tbsp flaxseeds

Directions:

1. Blend carrots and coconut water until smooth.
2. Add orange juice, grated ginger, flaxseeds and honey (if using).
3. Blend until all ingredients are well incorporated.

Useful Tip: Use frozen orange slices for a chilled smoothie.

Nutritional values: Calories: 90 kcal | Fat: 2 g | Protein: 3 g | Carbs: 18 g | Net carbs: 12 g | Fiber: 6 g | Cholesterol: 0 mg | Sodium: 60 mg | Potassium: 610 mg

AVOCADO SPINACH COCONUT SMOOTHIE

Serving: 4 | Prep time: 5 minutes | Cook time: 0 minutes

Ingredients:

- 1 ripe avocado, peeled and pitted
- 6 oz (170 g) fresh spinach leaves
- 8 oz (240 ml) coconut milk
- 8 oz (240 ml) unsweetened almond milk
- 2 tbsp unsweetened shredded coconut

Directions:

1. Blend spinach, coconut milk, and almond milk until smooth.
2. Add the avocado and shredded coconut.
3. Blend until the mixture is creamy and well combined.

Useful Tip: For added sweetness, consider adding a tablespoon of honey or a pitted date.

Nutritional values: Calories: 210 kcal | Fat: 18 g | Protein: 5 g | Carbs: 12 g | Net carbs: 5 g | Fiber: 7 g | Cholesterol: 0 mg | Sodium: 70 mg | Potassium: 660 mg

PEACH RASPBERRY CHIA SMOOTHIE

Serving: 4 | Prep time: 5 minutes | Cook time: 0 minutes

Ingredients:

- 12 oz (340 g) fresh or frozen peaches
- 8 oz (227 g) raspberries
- 16 oz (480 ml) unsweetened coconut water
- 2 tbsp chia seeds

Directions:

1. Blend peaches and coconut water until smooth.
2. Add raspberries and chia seeds.
3. Blend until all ingredients are thoroughly mixed.

Useful Tip: If using fresh fruit, consider adding a few ice cubes for a chilled smoothie.

Nutritional values: Calories: 90 kcal | Fat: 2 g | Protein: 3 g | Carbs: 18 g | Net carbs: 11 g | Fiber: 7 g | Cholesterol: 0 mg | Sodium: 20 mg | Potassium: 360 mg

BEETROOT ORANGE DETOX SMOOTHIE

Serving: 4 | Prep time: 5 minutes | Cook time: 0 minutes

Ingredients:

- 12 oz (340 g) cooked beetroot, chopped
- Juice of 4 oranges
- Zest of 1 orange
- 1-inch piece of ginger, peeled and chopped
- 12 oz (360 ml) coconut water

Directions:

1. Blend beetroot, coconut water, orange juice, orange zest, and ginger until smooth.
2. Add more coconut water if necessary for desired consistency.

Useful Tip: For added flavor, consider including a splash of lemon juice.

Nutritional values: Calories: 70 kcal | Fat: 0.5 g | Protein: 2 g | Carbs: 16 g | Net carbs: 12 g | Fiber: 4 g | Cholesterol: 0 mg | Sodium: 120 mg | Potassium: 540 mg

APPLE CINNAMON OATMEAL SMOOTHIE

Serving: 4 | Prep time: 5 minutes | Cook time: 0 minutes

Ingredients:

- 2 apples, peeled, cored, and chopped
- 4 oz (113 g) rolled oats
- 16 oz (480 ml) unsweetened almond milk
- 2 tbsp almond butter
- 2 tsp honey
- 1 tsp ground cinnamon
- 1/2 tsp vanilla extract

1. Blend chopped apples, rolled oats, almond milk, almond butter, honey, ground cinnamon, and vanilla extract until smooth.

2. Add more almond milk if a thinner consistency is preferred.

Useful Tip: For a thicker texture, consider adding a small amount of Greek yogurt or a frozen banana.

Nutritional values: Calories: 200 kcal | Fat: 7 g | Protein: 5 g | Carbs: 32 g | Net carbs: 25 g | Fiber: 7 g | Cholesterol: 0 mg | Sodium: 150 mg | Potassium: 360 mg

WATERMELON MINT HYDRATING SMOOTHIE

Serving: 4 | Prep time: 5 minutes | Cook time: 0 minutes

Ingredients:

- 20 oz (567 g) seedless watermelon, chopped
- 8 oz (240 ml) coconut water
- 2 oz (57 g) fresh mint leaves
- Juice of 2 limes
- 1 tbsp chia seeds
- 1 tsp agave syrup (optional)

Directions:

1. Blend chopped watermelon, coconut water, fresh mint leaves, lime juice, and chia seeds until smooth.

2. Add agave syrup if desired for additional sweetness.

Useful Tip: For a frostier texture, use frozen watermelon chunks instead of fresh ones.

Nutritional values: Calories: 80 kcal | Fat: 1 g | Protein: 2 g | Carbs: 18 g | Net carbs: 14 g | Fiber: 4 g | Cholesterol: 0 mg | Sodium: 10 mg | Potassium: 350 mg

DESSERTS

BAKED APPLE SLICES WITH CINNAMON

Serving: 4 | Prep time: 10 minutes | Cook time: 25 minutes

Ingredients:

- 4 medium-sized apples, cored and sliced
- 1 tbsp lemon juice
- 1 tbsp unsalted butter, melted
- 1 tbsp ground cinnamon
- 1 tbsp honey
- 2 tbsp chopped almonds
- 1 oz (28 g) rolled oats
- 1 oz (28 g) unsweetened applesauce

Directions:

1. Preheat the oven to 350°F (175°C).
2. In a bowl, toss the apple slices with lemon juice, melted butter, cinnamon, and honey until evenly coated.
3. Spread the apple slices on a baking sheet lined with parchment paper.
4. In a separate bowl, mix the chopped almonds, rolled oats, and applesauce.
5. Sprinkle the almond-oat mixture over the coated apple slices.
6. Bake for 20-25 minutes until the apples are tender and the topping is golden brown.

Useful Tip: These baked apple slices pair wonderfully with a dollop of unsweetened Greek yogurt for added creaminess and protein.

Nutritional values: Calories: 130 kcal | Fat: 4 g | Protein: 2 g | Carbs: 25 g | Net carbs: 19 g | Fiber: 6 g | Cholesterol: 5 mg | Sodium: 0 mg | Potassium: 220 mg

BANANA OATMEAL COOKIES

Serving: 4 | Prep time: 15 minutes | Cook time: 12 minutes

Ingredients:

- 2 ripe bananas, mashed
- 2 oz (57 g) almond flour
- 2 oz (57 g) rolled oats
- 1 tbsp coconut oil, melted
- 1 tbsp honey
- 1 tsp ground cinnamon
- 1/2 tsp vanilla extract
- 1 oz (28 g) chopped dates

Directions:

1. Preheat the oven to 350°F (175°C) and line a baking sheet with parchment paper.
2. In a bowl, combine mashed bananas, almond flour, rolled oats, melted coconut oil, honey, cinnamon, and vanilla extract until a dough forms.
3. Fold in the chopped dates until evenly distributed throughout the dough.

4. Scoop spoonfuls of dough onto the prepared baking sheet, flattening each slightly with a fork.

5. Bake for 10-12 minutes until the edges turn golden brown.

Useful Tip: Experiment with adding a sprinkle of unsweetened shredded coconut for an extra hint of flavor and texture.

Nutritional values: Calories: 150 kcal | Fat: 7 g | Protein: 3 g | Carbs: 21 g | Net carbs: 15 g | Fiber: 6 g | Cholesterol: 0 mg | Sodium: 0 mg | Potassium: 230 mg

ALMOND DATE ENERGY BITES

Serving: 4 | Prep time: 15 minutes | No cooking required

Ingredients:

- 2 oz (57 g) almonds
- 2 oz (57 g) rolled oats
- 2 oz (57 g) pitted dates
- 1 tbsp almond butter

- 1 tbsp honey
- 1 tsp vanilla extract
- 1/2 tsp ground cinnamon
- 1 oz (28 g) unsweetened shredded coconut

Directions:

1. In a food processor, pulse almonds and rolled oats until finely chopped.

2. Add pitted dates, almond butter, honey, vanilla extract, and ground cinnamon. Pulse until the mixture starts to come together.

3. Roll the mixture into bite-sized balls and coat each in shredded coconut.

4. Refrigerate the energy bites for at least 30 minutes before serving.

Useful Tip: For added crunch, consider rolling the energy bites in finely chopped pistachios or sesame seeds.

Nutritional values: Calories: 140 kcal | Fat: 7 g | Protein: 4 g | Carbs: 18 g | Net carbs: 11 g | Fiber: 7 g | Cholesterol: 0 mg | Sodium: 0 mg | Potassium: 210 mg

BERRY CHIA SEED PUDDING

Serving: 4 | Prep time: 10 minutes | Chill time: 2-3 hours

Ingredients:

- 4 oz (113 g) mixed berries (such as strawberries, blueberries, raspberries)
- 2 tbsp chia seeds
- 8 oz (240 ml) unsweetened almond milk

- 2 tbsp unsweetened shredded coconut
- 1 tbsp honey or maple syrup (optional)
- 1/2 tsp vanilla extract
- 1 oz (28 g) chopped almonds

Directions:

1. In a blender, pulse the mixed berries until pureed but slightly chunky.

2. In a mixing bowl, combine the berry puree, chia seeds, almond milk, shredded coconut, honey or maple syrup (if using), and vanilla extract. Mix well.

3. Cover and refrigerate for 2-3 hours or until the chia seeds have absorbed the liquid and the mixture thickens into a pudding-like consistency.

Useful Tip: Garnish the chia seed pudding with fresh berries and a sprinkle of chopped almonds for added texture and flavor.

Nutritional values: Calories: 110 kcal | Fat: 7 g | Protein: 3 g | Carbs: 10 g | Net carbs: 6 g | Fiber: 4 g | Cholesterol: 0 mg | Sodium: 40 mg | Potassium: 150 mg

PEACH AND YOGURT PARFAIT

Serving: 4 | Prep time: 10 minutes | Assembly time: 5 minutes

Ingredients:

- 2 ripe peaches, diced
- 8 oz (240 g) unsweetened Greek yogurt
- 2 oz (57 g) granola (sugar-free)
- 1 oz (28 g) chopped walnuts
- 1 tbsp honey (optional)
- 1/2 tsp cinnamon powder
- Fresh mint leaves for garnish

Directions:

1. In a bowl, mix diced peaches with honey (if using) and cinnamon powder.

2. In serving glasses or bowls, layer the peach mixture, Greek yogurt, and granola alternatively.

3. Top each parfait with a sprinkle of chopped walnuts and garnish with fresh mint leaves.

Useful Tip: Opt for plain, unsweetened Greek yogurt to minimize added sugars in this delightful parfait.

Nutritional values: Calories: 180 kcal | Fat: 9 g | Protein: 8 g | Carbs: 18 g | Net carbs: 12 g | Fiber: 6 g | Cholesterol: 0 mg | Sodium: 30 mg | Potassium: 260 mg

COCONUT MANGO RICE PUDDING

Serving: 4 | Prep time: 5 minutes | Cook time: 25 minutes

Ingredients:

- 4 oz (113 g) arborio rice
- 8 oz (240 ml) coconut milk (unsweetened)
- 2 ripe mangoes, diced
- 1 oz (28 g) unsweetened shredded coconut
- 2 tbsp honey or maple syrup
- 1/2 tsp vanilla extract
- Pinch of ground cardamom
- Chopped pistachios for garnish

Directions:

1. In a saucepan, combine arborio rice, coconut milk, diced mangoes, shredded coconut, honey or maple syrup, vanilla extract, and ground cardamom.

2. Bring the mixture to a gentle boil, then reduce the heat and let it simmer for 20-25 minutes, stirring occasionally, until the rice is cooked and the mixture thickens into a pudding-like consistency.

Useful Tip: Allow the rice pudding to cool slightly before serving; garnish each serving with chopped pistachios for a delightful crunch.

Nutritional values: Calories: 220 kcal | Fat: 7 g | Protein: 3 g | Carbs: 38 g | Net carbs: 32 g | Fiber: 6 g | Cholesterol: 0 mg | Sodium: 20 mg | Potassium: 340 mg

CHOCOLATE AVOCADO MOUSSE

Serving: 4 | Prep time: 5 minutes | Chill time: 1 hour

Ingredients:

- 2 ripe avocados
- 2 oz (57 g) unsweetened cocoa powder
- 2 oz (57 g) unsweetened almond milk
- 2 tbsp honey or maple syrup
- 1 tsp vanilla extract
- 1 oz (28 g) dark chocolate chips
- 1 oz (28 g) chopped almonds

Directions:

1. In a food processor, blend the avocados, cocoa powder, almond milk, honey or maple syrup, and vanilla extract until smooth.

2. Melt the dark chocolate chips and add them to the avocado mixture, pulsing until fully combined.

3. Transfer the mousse into serving cups and refrigerate for at least 1 hour.

Useful Tip: Top each serving with chopped almonds for a delightful crunch and added nutrition.

Nutritional values: Calories: 200 kcal | Fat: 15 g | Protein: 4 g | Carbs: 18 g | Net carbs: 10 g | Fiber: 8 g | Cholesterol: 0 mg | Sodium: 10 mg | Potassium: 590 mg

LEMON POPPY SEED MUFFINS

Serving: 4 | Prep time: 15 minutes | Bake time: 20 minutes

Ingredients:

- 4 oz (113 g) almond flour
- 2 oz (57 g) coconut flour
- 2 oz (57 g) unsweetened applesauce
- 2 oz (57 g) honey or maple syrup
- 2 oz (57 g) lemon juice
- 1 tsp baking powder
- 1 tbsp poppy seeds
- Lemon zest for garnish

Directions:

1. Preheat the oven to 350°F (175°C) and line a muffin tin with liners.
2. In a bowl, combine almond flour, coconut flour, applesauce, honey or maple syrup, lemon juice, baking powder, and poppy seeds. Mix until well combined.
3. Spoon the batter into the muffin cups, filling each about 2/3 full.
4. Bake for 18-20 minutes until the muffins are lightly golden and a toothpick inserted into the center comes out clean.

Useful Tip: Grate some fresh lemon zest on top of the muffins for a vibrant burst of citrus flavor.

Nutritional values: Calories: 190 kcal | Fat: 10 g | Protein: 4 g | Carbs: 20 g | Net carbs: 14 g | Fiber: 6 g | Cholesterol: 0 mg | Sodium: 10 mg | Potassium: 190 mg

BAKED PEAR WITH HONEY AND WALNUTS

Serving: 4 | Prep time: 15 minutes | Bake time: 20 minutes

Ingredients:

- 4 ripe pears, halved and cored
- 2 oz (57 g) chopped walnuts
- 2 oz (57 g) honey or maple syrup
- 1 tsp cinnamon powder
- 1 oz (28 g) unsalted butter

Directions:

1. Preheat the oven to 375°F (190°C) and line a baking dish with parchment paper.
2. Place the pear halves in the baking dish, cut side up.
3. In a bowl, mix chopped walnuts, honey or maple syrup, cinnamon, and unsalted butter. Spoon this mixture onto each pear half.
4. Bake for 18-20 minutes until the pears are tender and lightly caramelized.

Useful Tip: Serve the baked pears with a dollop of Greek yogurt for a delightful contrast of flavors and textures.

Nutritional values: Calories: 210 kcal | Fat: 12 g | Protein: 3 g | Carbs: 25 g | Net carbs: 18 g | Fiber: 7 g | Cholesterol: 15 mg | Sodium: 0 mg | Potassium: 300 mg

VANILLA BEAN PANNA COTTA

Serving: 4 | Prep time: 15 minutes | Chill time: 4 hours

Ingredients:

- 8 oz (240 ml) unsweetened almond milk
- 2 oz (57 g) gelatin powder
- 2 oz (57 g) honey or maple syrup
- 1 vanilla bean pod, seeds scraped
- 2 oz (57 g) chopped pistachios
- Fresh berries for garnish

Directions:

1. In a saucepan, heat almond milk until warm but not boiling. Remove from heat.

2. Stir in gelatin powder, honey or maple syrup, and scraped vanilla bean seeds until fully dissolved.

3. Pour the mixture into serving cups or molds and refrigerate for at least 4 hours or until set.

Useful Tip: Garnish each serving of panna cotta with chopped pistachios and fresh berries for added flavor and visual appeal.

Nutritional values: Calories: 150 kcal | Fat: 8 g | Protein: 5 g | Carbs: 15 g | Net carbs: 12 g | Fiber: 3 g | Cholesterol: 0 mg | Sodium: 30 mg | Potassium: 220 mg

MEAL PLAN

WEEK 1

DAYS	BREAKFAST	LUNCH	SNACK	DINNER
Day 1 Monday	Avocado Toast with Smoked Salmon	Lemon Herb Baked Salmon with Pomegranate Arugula Salad	Almond Butter Peaches Bites	Herbed Tilapia Fillets with Grilled Zucchini and Chickpea Salad
Day 2 Tuesday	Quinoa Breakfast Bowl with Mixed Berries	Garlic Butter Shrimp Skewers with Orange Almond Quinoa Salad	Roasted Cabbage with Herbs	Coconut Lime Mahi-Mahi with Broccoli Cranberry Slaw
Day 3 Wednesday	Spinach and Feta Omelette	Sesame Crusted Tuna Steaks with Apple Walnut Spinach Salad	Baked Sweet Potato Chips	Mediterranean Style Baked Red Snapper with Beetroot and Goat Cheese Salad
Day 4 Thursday	Mediterranean Veggie Scramble	Poached Cod with Tomato Salsa and Minty Watermelon Feta Salad	Cottage Cheese Stuffed Bell Peppers	Herb-Roasted Chicken Breast with Grilled Zucchini and Chickpea Salad
Day 5 Friday	Oatmeal with Cinnamon Apples and Walnuts	Lemon Dill Steamed Mussels with Pear and Walnut Mixed Greens Salad	Veggie Sticks with Hummus Dip	Lemon Herb Grilled Chicken Skewers with Orange Almond Quinoa Salad
Day 6 Saturday	Sweet Potato Hash with Turkey Sausage	Baked Haddock with Herbed Crust and Broccoli Cranberry Slaw	Roasted Carrot and Lentil Salad	Rosemary Baked Chicken Thighs with Pomegranate Arugula Salad
Day 7 Sunday	Whole Grain Pancakes with Blueberry Compote	Herb-Crusted Baked Halibut with Grilled Zucchini and Chickpea Salad	Apple Walnut Spinach Salad	Herb Roasted Monkfish Tail with Minty Watermelon Feta Salad

WEEK 2

DAYS	BREAKFAST	LUNCH	SNACK	DINNER
Day 1 Monday	Whole Grain Pancakes with Blueberry Compote	Baked Haddock with Herbed Crust and Minty Watermelon Feta Salad	Veggie Sticks with Hummus Dip	Lemon Herb Baked Salmon with Pear and Walnut Mixed Greens Salad
Day 2 Tuesday	Avocado Toast with Smoked Salmon	Herb-Roasted Chicken Breast with Orange Almond Quinoa Salad	Roasted Carrot and Lentil Salad	Sesame Crusted Tuna Steaks with Apple Walnut Spinach Salad
Day 3 Wednesday	Apple Cinnamon Buckwheat Porridge	Lemon Dill Steamed Mussels with Pomegranate Arugula Salad	Almond Butter Peaches Bites	Coconut Lime Mahi-Mahi with Grilled Zucchini and Chickpea Salad
Day 4 Thursday	Veggie-packed Breakfast Frittata	Garlic Butter Shrimp Skewers with Beetroot and Goat Cheese Salad	Cottage Cheese Stuffed Bell Peppers	Rosemary Baked Chicken Thighs with Broccoli Cranberry Slaw
Day 5 Friday	Breakfast Burrito with Black Beans and Salsa	Lemon Herb Grilled Chicken Skewers with Minty Watermelon Feta Salad	Baked Sweet Potato Chips	Lemon Dill Steamed Mussels with Orange Almond Quinoa Salad
Day 6 Saturday	Mediterranean Veggie Scramble	Sesame Crusted Tuna Steaks with Grilled Zucchini and Chickpea Salad	Beetroot and Goat Cheese Salad	Herb-Crusted Baked Halibut with Pomegranate Arugula Salad
Day 7 Sunday	Spinach and Feta Omelette	Lemon Herb Baked Salmon with Pear and Walnut Mixed Greens Salad	Orange Almond Quinoa Salad	Garlic Butter Shrimp Skewers with Broccoli Cranberry Slaw

WEEK 3

DAYS	BREAKFAST	LUNCH	SNACK	DINNER
Day 1 Monday	Veggie-packed Breakfast Frittata	Lemon Garlic Grilled Turkey Cutlets with Pomegranate Arugula Salad	Roasted Cabbage with Herbs	Herb-Crusted Baked Halibut with Minty Watermelon Feta Salad
Day 2 Tuesday	Apple Cinnamon Buckwheat Porridge	Garlic Butter Shrimp Skewers with Orange Almond Quinoa Salad	Cottage Cheese Stuffed Bell Peppers	Rosemary Baked Chicken Thighs with Pear and Walnut Mixed Greens Salad
Day 3 Wednesday	Breakfast Burrito with Black Beans and Salsa	Coconut Lime Mahi-Mahi with Broccoli Cranberry Slaw	Baked Sweet Potato Chips	Lemon Dill Steamed Mussels with Grilled Zucchini and Chickpea Salad
Day 4 Thursday	Mediterranean Veggie Scramble	Herb-Roasted Chicken Breast with Beetroot and Goat Cheese Salad	Almond Butter Peaches Bites	Sesame Crusted Tuna Steaks with Apple Walnut Spinach Salad
Day 5 Friday	Spinach and Feta Omelette	Herbed Tilapia Fillets with Minty Watermelon Feta Salad	Pear and Walnut Mixed Greens Salad	Lemon Herb Grilled Chicken Skewers with Orange Almond Quinoa Salad
Day 6 Saturday	Sweet Potato Hash with Turkey Sausage	Mediterranean Style Baked Red Snapper with Grilled Zucchini and Chickpea Salad	Beetroot and Goat Cheese Salad	Herb Roasted Monkfish Tail with Roasted Cabbage with Herbs
Day 7 Sunday	Quinoa Breakfast Bowl with Mixed Berries	Poached Cod with Tomato Salsa and Broccoli Cranberry Slaw	Orange Almond Quinoa Salad	Garlic Butter Shrimp Skewers with Pomegranate Arugula Salad

WEEK 4

DAYS	BREAKFAST	LUNCH	SNACK	DINNER
Day 1 Monday	Mediterranean Veggie Scramble	Lemon Garlic Grilled Turkey Cutlets with Pomegranate Arugula Salad	Roasted Cabbage with Herbs	Herb-Crusted Baked Halibut with Minty Watermelon Feta Salad
Day 2 Tuesday	Avocado Toast with Smoked Salmon	Garlic Butter Shrimp Skewers with Orange Almond Quinoa Salad	Cottage Cheese Stuffed Bell Peppers	Rosemary Baked Chicken Thighs with Pear and Walnut Mixed Greens Salad
Day 3 Wednesday	Breakfast Burrito with Black Beans and Salsa	Coconut Lime Mahi-Mahi with Broccoli Cranberry Slaw	Baked Sweet Potato Chips	Lemon Dill Steamed Mussels with Grilled Zucchini and Chickpea Salad
Day 4 Thursday	Mediterranean Veggie Scramble	Herb-Roasted Chicken Breast with Beetroot and Goat Cheese Salad	Almond Butter Peaches Bites	Sesame Crusted Tuna Steaks with Apple Walnut Spinach Salad
Day 5 Friday	Spinach and Feta Omelette	Herbed Tilapia Fillets with Minty Watermelon Feta Salad	Pear and Walnut Mixed Greens Salad	Lemon Herb Grilled Chicken Skewers with Orange Almond Quinoa Salad
Day 6 Saturday	Sweet Potato Hash with Turkey Sausage	Mediterranean Style Baked Red Snapper with Grilled Zucchini and Chickpea Salad	Beetroot and Goat Cheese Salad	Herb Roasted Monkfish Tail with Roasted Cabbage with Herbs
Day 7 Sunday	Quinoa Breakfast Bowl with Mixed Berries	Poached Cod with Tomato Salsa and Broccoli Cranberry Slaw	Orange Almond Quinoa Salad	Garlic Butter Shrimp Skewers with Pomegranate Arugula Salad

CONCLUSION

Embarking on the Fatty Liver Diet journey marks a significant step toward nurturing and supporting your liver health for a better quality of life. Through this journey, you've gained valuable insights into crafting a diet and lifestyle that supports your liver and overall well-being.

Empowerment Through Knowledge

Understanding the impact of diet, exercise, and lifestyle on liver health empowers you to make informed choices. You've learned that a balanced diet rich in liver-friendly foods, coupled with portion control and mindful meal planning, forms the cornerstone of managing fatty liver disease.

Lifestyle as a Foundation

Lifestyle modifications, including regular exercise, stress management, and sufficient sleep, serve as a strong foundation for a healthy liver. These changes extend beyond mere dietary adjustments, fostering a holistic approach to well-being.

Navigating Challenges and Achieving Balance

Addressing obstacles like cravings, social situations, and potential pitfalls has equipped you with strategies to navigate challenges while staying committed to your goals. It's not about perfection but finding a balance that supports your liver health while allowing flexibility.

Seeking Support and Progress Monitoring

Seeking professional guidance and support networks have been emphasized to ensure your journey is well-guided and supported. Monitoring progress through various means, whether tracking dietary habits or regular health check-ups, helps assess and adjust your approach.

Embracing Long-Term Commitment

The Fatty Liver Diet isn't just a short-term fix; it's a lifestyle that fosters long-term liver health. Consistency, patience, and gradual changes are the keys to sustainable progress and maintaining the positive outcomes achieved.

Continuing the Journey

As you conclude this chapter, remember that your journey towards optimal liver health continues. Continue to embrace the principles learned, personalize your approach, and seek ongoing support to ensure a fulfilling and healthy lifestyle.

By implementing these lessons and principles from the Fatty Liver Diet Cookbook, you've taken significant strides toward nurturing your liver health. Your dedication and commitment to this journey pave the way for a healthier, happier life ahead.

TABLE OF MEASUREMENT UNITS

INGREDIENT	CUPS	GRAMS	OUNCES
All-Purpose Flour	1 cup	120g	4.2 oz
Whole Wheat Flour	1 cup	130g	4.6 oz
Granulated Sugar	1 cup	200g	7.1 oz
Brown Sugar	1 cup	220g	7.8 oz
Powdered Sugar	1 cup	120g	4.2 oz
Butter	1 cup	227g	8 oz
Olive Oil	1 cup	216g	7.6 oz
Milk	1 cup	240g	8.5 oz
Water	1 cup	240g	8.5 oz
Honey	1 cup	340g	12 oz
Yogurt	1 cup	240g	8.5 oz
Rice (uncooked)	1 cup	185g	6.5 oz
Pasta (uncooked)	1 cup	140g	4.9 oz
Quinoa (uncooked)	1 cup	185g	6.5 oz
Lentils (uncooked)	1 cup	200g	7.1 oz
Chickpeas (canned)	1 cup	240g	8.5 oz
Almonds	1 cup	140g	4.9 oz
Walnuts	1 cup	125g	4.4 oz

INGREDIENT	CUPS	GRAMS	OUNCES
Tomatoes (diced)	1 cup	240g	8.5 oz
Cucumbers (sliced)	1 cup	119g	4.2 oz
Bell Peppers	1 cup	149g	5.3 oz
Spinach (fresh)	1 cup	30g	1.1 oz
Basil (fresh)	1 cup	21g	0.7 oz
Feta Cheese	1 cup	150g	5.3 oz
Greek Yogurt	1 cup	245g	8.6 oz
Olives (pitted)	1 cup	180g	6.3 oz
Honey	1 cup	340g	12 oz
Red Wine Vinegar	1 cup	240g	8.5 oz
Lemon Juice	1 cup	240g	8.5 oz
Balsamic Vinegar	1 cup	240g	8.5 oz
Hummus	1 cup	240g	8.5 oz
Tahini	1 cup	240g	8.5 oz
Greek Salad Dressing	1 cup	240g	8.5 oz

Limitation of Liability / Disclaimer of Warranty: The publisher and the author of this work are not medical professionals and do not provide medical counseling, treatments, or diagnoses. The contents of this work are provided for informational purposes only and should not be considered a substitute for professional medical advice. The publisher and the author make no warranties or representations regarding the accuracy or completeness of the information presented herein. The information in this work has not been evaluated by the U.S. Food and Drug Administration, and it is not intended to diagnose, treat, cure, or prevent any disease. It is recommended that individuals seek full medical clearance from a licensed physician before initiating any diet or health-related practices. The advice and strategies presented in this work may not be suitable for every individual, and the publisher and the author disclaim any responsibility for any adverse effects or consequences resulting from the use, application, or interpretation of the information provided.

Nutritional Information: The nutritional information provided in this work is based on specific brands, measurements, and ingredients used in the recipes. It is intended for informational purposes only and should not be considered a guarantee of the actual nutritional value of the reader's prepared recipe. The publisher and the author are not responsible for any damages or losses resulting from reliance on the provided nutritional information.

Made in the USA
Coppell, TX
16 September 2024

37334439R00046